Learning to Listen

OTHER BOOKS BY WENDY MILLER

Men of Revival in Germany
(Translated from Ernst Modersohn)

Advent Poems & Devotional Guide
(Published privately)

Learning to Listen

A GUIDE FOR SPIRITUAL FRIENDS

Wendy Miller

UPPER ROOM BOOKS
Nashville

LEARNING TO LISTEN
©1993 Wendy Miller.
All Rights Reserved.

Unless otherwise designated, scripture quotations are from the *New
Revised Standard Version,* © 1989 by the Division of Christian Education
of the National Council of Churches of Christ in the United States of
America, and are used by permission.

Scripture quotations designated TEV are from the *Good News Bible,* The
Bible In Today's English Version - Old Testament: Copyright ©
American Bible Society 1976; New Testament: Copyright © American
Bible Society 1966, 1971, 1976.

[··]
Cover design: Leigh Ann Dans (Nashville)
ISBN 0-8358-0677-4
Library of Congress Catalog Card Number: 92-61441
First printing: March 1993 (5)
Printed in the USA.

FOR ED
whose love enables me to listen
and
FOR MY CHILDREN AND GRANDCHILDREN
who help me see God
in the everyday

[··]

Finding Your Way

[··]

Early in his ministry Jesus invited persons to be with him on his journey. Mark tells us that Jesus formed a rhythm in his relationship with his disciples—a rhythm of coming, of being with, and of responding:

> [Jesus] went up the mountain and called to him those whom he wanted, and they came to him. . . . to be with him, and to be sent out.
> —Mark 3:13, 14, NRSV

We tend to focus on the responding—the sending forth "into all the world" of Mark 16. But Jesus included all three movements in the life of his followers: turning aside from our activity to come to Jesus, learning to be with him, and then responding to him as Jesus guides us on our outward journey. This time "with Jesus" puts us in the place where we learn to listen.

[··]

These three movements are the pattern you are invited to follow in your personal times in the quiet, in your journey outward, and also in your times with your spiritual friend.

PART ONE of *Learning to Listen* gives you an idea of what spiritual friendship is about and helps you on the journey to finding such a friend. At the end of this section, a guide is given for your times together as spiritual friends. You may want to refer to this section from time to time as you learn to listen to and with each other.

PART TWO gives some guidance along the path of beginning a spiritual friendship.

PART THREE contains a suggested guide for your personal time in the quiet and some help to lead you into practicing several spiritual disciplines. The disciplines are also described in a way that adapts to the movements of coming, being with, and responding on the outward journey.

PART FOUR is a reading guide based on Matthew's Gospel. It will be helpful for you to read PART THREE before moving into the reading guide since it refers to the spiritual disciplines described there. While readings are suggested for five days of each of thirteen weeks, feel free to move at your own pace.

PART FIVE contains a helpful, simple, and practical guide to maintaining a spiritual friendship.

[··]

Jesus continues to call us into the quiet of his presence, but we do not need to walk alone. Discovering another disciple whom Jesus has also called, and listening to what Jesus is saying in the times of being with him or her is what spiritual friendship is all about. I invite the spirit of Jesus to guide you on your journey.

Wendy Miller
HARRISONBURG, VIRGINIA

[*PART ONE*]

Spiritual Friendship

[··]

CHAPTER 1

Who Is a Spiritual Friend?

[··]

Marjorie had invited us to do some remembering. There were about twelve of us seated in the circle of chairs, participating in a faith nurture workshop designed to help us understand and use the new curriculum for children and adolescents in our local congregation.

"Think back over your life," she explained. "Reflect on those people and experiences that have influenced your faith development as a child, an adolescent, and an adult."

After some time in the silence, my attention wandered back to my early teens. I could remember kneeling beside a big, old, iron-railed bed in the room I slept in when I was fourteen; praying that God would bring our family back together and that we would have a place of our own to live. The house where we were staying belonged to friends of my mother's. It was our third temporary home in six months following the splintering of my parents' marriage and the scattering of our family.

I remembered looking up at the brass light fixture hanging in the center of the high ceiling, wondering if my prayers floated up that far only to drop back down to the worn carpet on the floor. God seemed distant. And from my teenage perspective, nothing seemed to ever change.

I also remembered the brief but significant nudgings I felt here and there during those early teen years, usually when I was not praying. There were some words from a hymn expressing love for Jesus written on a scrap of paper, which in some strange way had turned up beside my locker at school. I felt a stab of guilt because I was not ready to love Jesus, but deeper within myself I knew that a willingness toward Jesus was being asked of me. Sometimes when I stood outside looking at the night sky punctuated with stars, I seemed to be given an inner knowing that encountering God was bound up with my life, with anyone's life. At the time I did not realize that God was trying to get my attention. All I knew was that I was not ready to encounter God. That would probably have other consequences, perhaps allowing Jesus to make demands. My response at the time was resistance.

Later that evening at the workshop, over a cup of tea, I reminisced with Marjorie about that fourteen-year-old memory. She listened carefully, and then in her insightful way, asked: "Have you ever thought that maybe God was the One drawing you to pray in your pain? Or that your question about God's being distant was the beginning of a conversation God was wanting to have with you?"

Marjorie was not only creating space for us to pay attention to our faith journey, she was also listening as a spiritual friend as I reflected on my experience of God and my response to God in that period of my life. I began to see that the grief and loneliness of that time was also an opening onto something new and life-giving, rather than just a miserable memory. I could also see that the loneliness I had felt because of the separation within my family was an echo of that deeper loneliness we all experience—the loneliness that comes from being apart from God, from our inner self, and from one another.

[··]

Spiritual friends are people who pay attention, with another person, to the presence and the movement of God in that person's life; and to the response the other person is making to God, to him or herself, to others, and to God's creation. Such friends come in all shapes and sizes and show up in a variety of places and times in our lives. Several spiritual friends appeared and helped the apostle Paul as he began his Christian pilgrimage. Ananias had the courage to explain to Paul that it was the Lord Jesus who had appeared to him on his journey to Damascus and who would also help Paul see and be filled with the Holy Spirit.[1] Barnabas paid attention to the Jerusalem disciples' resistance to and fear of God's working in Paul's life. He facilitated a place for Paul and the others to meet and to embrace the grace of God among them.[2]

Persons with the gift of being an evangelist can be a spiritual friend. Philip was open and sensitive to the spiritual search of the Ethiopian court treasurer. His sensitivity, born out of his ability to listen attentively to the Spirit of God, enabled Philip to discern where the Ethiopian was in his experience and to listen to his questions.[3] Our questions can also be signals of where God is at work in our lives.

Irene Bergg, an elderly, white-haired woman who led a Bible class for teenage girls, was that kind of spiritual friend for me. Irene prayed for me, wrote to me, and when my family did move for the fourth and final time into a home of our own, became the friend who paid attention to where I was on my journey home to God. I began paying attention to God as the Holy Spirit moved gently in the world of my questions about who Jesus was, what his life and death meant, and what meaning Christ's return had for me. With the gentleness, patience, and skill of a midwife, Irene Bergg attended to the birthing of spiritual life in me and helped me to embrace Jesus Christ, the Spring and Giver of life and the Way home to God.

[··]

Ever since the first man and woman in Eden chose to chase after a web of illusions spun by the great enemy of God and all of God's creation, we find that we are not at home; we are distant from God, from our self, and from one another. We no longer enjoy the harmony and community of Eden. It is this alienation, the colossal divorce we all suffer, that fuels our anxiety and our addiction for something to fill the painful space within us and between us. Much of what we do is only a continual effort to drown the pain, to cram the space full with whatever the latest fad might be—even religious fads. But the space belongs to God and God alone.

We tend to interpret the longing we feel as a need to try something new, something else. But the longings are God-given, spirit-breathed:

As a deer longs for flowing streams,
so my soul longs for you, O God.
My soul thirsts for God,
for the living God.
When shall I come and behold
the face of God?[4]

When we do begin to take notice of our daily rush and stress, when we begin here and there to wish that life would somehow be other—these are God moments in our journey. God nudges past our compulsive race to keep up with others and creates a quiet space for the healing song of the Holy Spirit to resonate with the longing of our inner spirit.

Digestion of such fleeting awareness is crucial. The whole authentic history of spiritual discipline in the Church and in all deep religious traditions is to aid human digestion of the Holy, so that we do not 1) reject its nourishment 2) throw it up by not allowing room inside for it 3) mistake "artificial flavors" for the real thing 4) use its strength for building an ego empire, . . . rather than for sharing in myriad form for the good of others. [5]

In his letter to the believers in Philippi, Paul helps them to see that God who had begun the good work of grace in their lives would also be continuing this spiritual activity in them.[6] This transforming work of God happens as Christ is formed in us.[7]

A spiritual friend can help us pay attention to this transforming work of faith, hope, and love. Sometimes a pastor or a Sunday school teacher is able to assist us in this way. Eugene Peterson, pastor, writer, and spiritual friend, observes that most people assume that pastors are:

teaching people to pray, helping parishioners discern the presence of grace in events and feelings, affirming the presence of God at the very heart of life, sharing a search for light through a dark passage in the pilgrimage, guiding the formation of a self-understanding that is biblically spiritual instead of merely psychological or sociological.[8]

However, one does not have to be a pastor to be attentive to God and what God is doing. My family doctor, after gently examining a painful injury to my eye, remarked kindly: "While you are lying still, waiting for healing, always remember that you are as close to God as your eyeball is to you. Everything you suffer, God feels with you. Remember with the psalmist that you are the apple of God's eye." His awareness of God's presence in my suffering and in the dark space of waiting for healing helped me to open my attention to God on a far deeper level than the healing of my eye.

CHAPTER 2

Spontaneous Encounters

[··]

The conversations with Marjorie and my family doctor were some of those unplanned, occasional encounters with a spiritual friend. At the time I did not recognize either of these persons as such, but as I was reflecting on those persons who had in some way paid attention to God's presence in my life, I realized what insight they had given me. My doctor's understanding helped me to see my pain as a place to experience God's care. Then there was the gift of a window Marjorie had given me through her questions —a window inviting me to look in on the delicate movement of the Holy Spirit during my adolescence and to see what my response to that stirring had been.

Such conversations may happen more often than we realize. Bits of the holy are imbedded in the everyday, but most of us fail to recognize our encounter with God for what it is. We may think such meetings only happen at church, rather than in the supermarket, in our backyard, or while we are waiting for transportation.[9]

[··]

We were in Belgium, and while my husband, Ed, and our son, Mark, inquired about a rental car, I was watching our luggage on the sidewalk in front of the ferry dock in Ostende. Two other travelers carried their suitcases into the July sun and set them down near mine. As we waited, Barry told me he was a university student from Iowa. He had just missed the train to Frankfurt, Germany, from where he would fly back to the United States, and he was waiting for another connection. Maria was from Luxembourg and was also waiting for a train. Noontime came as Ed and Mark returned with the rental car, and Barry and Maria accepted our invitation to join us for a picnic lunch before we journeyed on to the Netherlands.

Over sandwiches, fruit, and soft drinks, Barry kept us entertained with stories of his European adventures. He had expected to spend the three months with his brother, but after his arrival at the airport in Frankfurt, his brother informed Barry that he had other plans. So Barry had decided to explore Europe on his own. Two weeks later, while he was in Berlin, all his luggage was stolen. In Spain he slept on the streets along with a score of other tourists, hoping to see the bull runs the next day. Any sleep Barry managed to catch was interrupted by an icy blast of water at five the next morning; the city officials were clearing the streets of loiterers with a fire hose. Barry continued to entertain us with his stories and his humor as we ate.

After listening for some time, I asked: "Barry, how did you survive? Where did you find whatever it took to come through all this? I'm not sure that, when I was your age, I could have endured all that you have with such humor and bounce."

He paused for a few moments and then his voice softened. "My family used to be in a lot of chaos," he said. "My parents were alcoholics, and we grew distant from any church connection we had. I finally went to Al-Anon and learned to pray. My parents also got some help, and we found a warm group of people in a congregation we could begin over with. The book I used to read to help me open up to God got stolen with my luggage, but I know I'm not alone," he concluded quietly.

The early afternoon bustle of feet on the sidewalk, the rush of traffic on the street in front of the ferry terminal, the snatches of conversation from passersby receded into the distance. The space we sat in felt holy. We had become aware of God.

[··]

Persons often become aware of God in times of crisis or when they are ill or when the group support they depend on (family or friends) is no longer available. It is at such times as these that unplanned encounters with spiritual friends can happen. Sometimes these spontaneous interactions can be the basis for a longer relationship.

CHAPTER 3

Finding a Spiritual Friend

[··]

Today there is a renewal of the long tradition in the church for intentional spiritual friendship. In the face of "frenzied, confused, everybody-working, emotionally and materially distracted and often broken family settings that increasingly dominate our culture,"[10] we are feeling a need for the kind of friend:

> who can be with us not only through crisis, but through the more mundane times of spiritual attentiveness in our lives. Proliferation of such friendships perhaps can help shape, deepen, and stabilize the shallow spiritual infrastructure of the Church, aiding its renewal and unique service to society. . . . such friendships do not require spiritual masters, just attentive faithful companions.[11]

Sometimes we are aware of God's intervention in times of crisis, and we remember such times with thankfulness and joy.

Campfire meetings and testimony times ring with such memories. But a spiritual friend helps us notice God's loving presence in the everydayness of life.

[··]

Arthur was happily married, had two lovely sons, and enjoyed his work. He and Sally felt at home in the community where they lived and in the congregation where they were members. On the surface Art knew he had everything going for him. Recently however, he felt the need for something more. He and Sally knew they were involved in more community and church activities than they really wanted, but there did not seem to be time to think about where all of this constant motion was taking them or their children. Although it was gratifying to be well liked and respected by his friends and peers, Art had to admit that he was tired of so much busyness. And when he thought about his prayer life, it felt like a desert.

His pastor began to notice that Art was not the only man in the congregation who found little time to pay attention to his spiritual life. He decided to offer an evening gathering for men who would be interested in deepening their discipleship. As part of the experience, the pastor invited the men to pair up and make a commitment to meet and share their life and spiritual awareness together. Art and Stan decided they could meet once a month over breakfast on Saturday morning. As Art began paying attention to his prayer life, he felt a growing freedom to think about letting go of those responsibilities that kept him busier than he knew was healthy for him or for his family.

Jenny had just completed a women's Bible study course and noticed how her spiritual attentiveness had developed as she experienced the prayer and scripture meditations. But now that the course was over, Jenny felt the need for some continued kind of structure or accountability. When she noticed a Sunday school class on spiritual friendship being offered, Jenny decided to attend. As part of the course, persons were invited to consider finding a spiritual friend with whom to share their pilgrimage. After praying for some help and guidance, Jenny decided to get in touch with a woman she knew in another congregation. They began by meeting every two weeks.

Dan had taught school ever since he had graduated from college and had been active in the church. Now that he was retiring from teaching he had more time for his part-time pastoral work, and he began to reflect on what direction his ministry would take. He had read books about prayer for years. "I always thought that the good feelings I had when I read a book about prayer were some kind of indication of my love for God and my Christian growth," he told me one day during a visit at the seminary. "But as I was reading Andrew Murray, he quoted some words from William Law about thinking that when we read something and feel energized and excited about what we have read, then we are to watch out. Law says that the good feelings can lead us into thinking that we possess what we have read, when in actuality they are only good thoughts and feelings."[12] Dan paused for a moment, then continued. "Those words caught my attention," he said. "I thought about the many times I've had good thoughts and feelings as I read about prayer. But I'm beginning to realize that that did not change me over the long haul. Prayer has to do with meeting God."

Dan and I continued to reflect on his insight about prayer's being more than an occasion to bring requests and thanksgivings to God. Rather, we were learning that prayer is our response to God's invitation to turn from where our attention is held captive and to open our awareness to God who is present at all times. Then Dan told me about his desire for spiritual friendship. "I invited any person in my congregation who was interested to meet with me once a month to talk about our spiritual life together. So far, three persons have indicated an interest."

[··]

You may be wondering just how to go about finding a spiritual friend or a small group committed to helping each other pay attention to God's presence in our lives and assisting each other to recognize our reactions and responses to God. While such friendships are beginning to emerge, the rediscovery of the ancient and biblical practice of spiritual or soul friendship is still new enough to you that you may be unsure of where to look or how to start looking.

Begin by praying, by asking for God's help in your quest. You may find it helpful to spend time in quiet, waiting before God; first telling God about your desire, and then waiting in the stillness to hear what God has to share with you. You may find the name of someone coming to mind. You may wait in the silence and find that nothing comes to mind. In either case, your journey has begun and is being assisted by God. Trust the spirit of God to guide you in your search.

As you wait, as you continue to pray and be attentive to the thoughts and suggestions moving into your awareness, in time you will probably find some persons' names coming to mind. Some may be more known to you, and with others you may not have such a close acquaintance.

[··]

Gwen had just moved into a new town and felt the need for a spiritual friend. She knew very few people in the local community or in the congregation she decided to attend. During those early months of adjustment, Gwen began praying for God's help in her search. After some time she felt drawn to a woman in the congregation, a person she had met only briefly, but someone who seemed to care about prayer and the inner life of discipleship. Gwen decided to ask Adelle if she would meet over a cup of tea to talk about spiritual friendship. As it happened, the woman with whom Adelle had enjoyed meeting for spiritual friendship for some years had recently moved, and Adelle was also praying for someone else to meet with. A new friendship was begun.

[..]

It is my experience that I find what I look for. I begin to notice what I am paying attention to—whether it be yellow crocuses bursting through the snow in March, or God's invitations to come and listen scattered throughout the Bible story. When I began my own search for a spiritual friend, I became aware of others who were interested in the same soul journey.

CHAPTER 4

Qualities of a Spiritual Friend

[··]

"I have a spiritual friend," Doug said. "We meet pretty often and talk about all kinds of spiritual subjects." My husband, Ed, and I were enjoying an after-dinner visit with some friends, and after a while the conversation around the table began to focus on our experience of God. Doug continued: "We talk about God. We discuss prophecy and what the scriptures are saying."

As we listened, we realized that Doug's experience was very similar to ours and other persons. I remembered the long conversations I had enjoyed with friends over the years. Sometimes they took place as we were driving somewhere; more often they were around the table after a meal. All kinds of spiritual subjects were discussed, concerns aired, positions and convictions stated.

What I began to realize in time was that very few, if any, of our conversations rested comfortably in our awareness of God and how God's presence in our lives was shaping our response to God, to ourselves, and to others. Another piece was also missing: careful, quiet listening. I did hear a person's ideas, but often I was thinking of what I would like to say next. Seldom did I hear or pay attention to the inner concerns of the other. For that kind of listening, we need to slow down, lay our own agenda aside, and be fully present to the other. We also need to begin paying attention to our own inner world. As we become more comfortable with the multicolored movement within ourselves, we are able to be present to another as she tries to express her inner experience in words.

As you think about both being and finding a spiritual friend, consider the following qualities:

1. An ability to listen, to be attentive.
2. An ability to provide hospitality: making space for another to enter and be at home as he or she lays a piece of his or her inner life out for another to see.
3. Trust and acceptance: "Someone with whom you feel free to unlock your heart and trust, and who will be able to help you focus . . . on your spiritual journey."[13]
4. A willingness to be accountable.
5. A willingness to pray and to allow one's life to be changed and transformed through the grace of God.
6. An openness to God and the movement of God's spirit.
7. A sense of humor.

This search is a journey in itself. You may be blessed with the gift of a soul friend early in your quest. Often the search takes a little longer. My first experience of finding a spiritual friend took two years. Part of that length of time was due to the fact that I was not completely sure just what spiritual friendship was about or what questions could help me in my search. But my journey also took longer because I was resisting the risk of revealing my inner self to another.

CHAPTER 5

Resistance

[··]

As we consider connecting with a spiritual friend, we may well discover some hesitation within. Our spiritual life emerges from the depths of who we are. If we bring its movements into the light of another's gaze, what might happen?

Like Adam and Eve in Eden, we fear being discovered. We are also fearful of change.

> I might be led to change my way of seeing and behaving. There is something in us that stubbornly resists this possibility . . . . Why not let corporate worship, personal prayer, and my own discernment be sufficient?[14]

If we are honest with ourselves, we have to admit that we like to be in control.

I procrastinated. It didn't take me long to get to the root of my reluctance: I didn't want to share what was most essential to me. I wanted to keep control. I wanted to be boss . . . . What I detected in myself was . . . a battle with spiritual pride.[15]

Such fears tend to keep us in bondage to a self-induced isolation and move us further from the sense of community God invites us to enter. In choosing a friend to whom you will entrust your soul journey, you will find yourself confronting these fears with new courage—the courage to trust. "Only those do we call friends to whom we can fearlessly entrust our heart and all its secrets; those too, who in turn, are bound to us by the same law of faith and security."[16] This trust grows within the safe soil of a mutual covenant based in love, patient acceptance, confession, and obedience to Christ. As the hard shell of fear softens, the roots of trust and faith grow, and the gracious home for God, our true selves, and others blossoms in us and around us.

We are assisting in the continual birthing of spiritual life in the other, a birth that happens in its own time. We cannot push the pace of grace. Rather, a loving and patient sensitivity is called for on our part to be with the other as a friend, always aware that the same birthing is happening in ourselves as we surrender ourselves to the movement and transformation of the spirit of God within us.

As we learn to be present to God, to open our attention to the God who is present to us, and to be aware of when we are not attentive and resistant to being present, then we will be more able to pick up on such movements in another. We are pilgrims together on the journey of the soul. We are learning to become aware of when we lose our place and of our need for a friend to direct us to the signposts God is offering.

PART TWO

Meeting with a Spiritual Friend

[..]

CHAPTER 6

Beginning a Spiritual Friendship

[··]

There may come a time when you are feeling ready to approach someone about entering into a mutual journey of soul friendship—whether one on one or in a small group. This is when you will find it helpful to meet together and explore the possibilities.

If you are deciding to use a guide such as this or another, or even if you are deciding to be more non-structured, your covenant for spiritual friendship can grow out of your discussion and decisions concerning the following questions.

How often are we able and willing to meet?
Some persons meet each week, others every two or three weeks, and some once a month. I know of some spiritual

friends who are not able to meet monthly but telephone and write to each other to stay in touch.

How long should our meetings be?
If both of you are going to be sharing your journey, you may need more than an hour.

Where will we meet?
Some spiritual friends meet in a quiet area of a restaurant over a cup of tea or a meal.

Others like to meet where there is privacy and quiet— free from interruption from the phone or other intrusions. For some this can be in a living room, for others a quiet room in a church. Some persons prefer to go for a walk in the park or some other scenic area.

What kind of time commitment can we make to begin?
This handbook is designed for a three-month journey— enough time to know if you are beginning to feel comfortable with each other and to decide if you would like to continue or discontinue meeting. This kind of trial period will give you the freedom and space to know if any tension stems from your own fear of disclosure or from a sense that the relationship is not working.[17]

CHAPTER 7

Your Times Together

[··]

The conversation of spiritual friends covers all of life since how we relate to God finally affects every other part of who we are, how we relate to ourselves and others, and what we do.

As you begin your journey as spiritual friends together, you need to spend some time talking about how the journey will be similar to other forms of friendship and how will it be different. Such conversations assist you in being open and honest about what kind of boundaries you will need to set.

This kind of discussion and covenant will free you to move within the boundaries you have agreed on. Seek to be open and honest with each other concerning what you need and what is appropriate or inappropriate. This is part of the process of building and maintaining trust. Agree to confront each other in love if you stray beyond the boundaries of the covenant you have set.

One other note: This chapter will give some guidance for how to listen. The section entitled *Preparing for Your Time Together* in the READING GUIDE also offers some suggestions.

Preparation for Your Times Together

Along with your arrangements for when and where you will meet, keep your friend in your prayers. Pray also about your time together.

To help create and protect the space for listening, you will probably find it helpful to decide who will be the "gatekeeper." Sometimes one of the partners is more naturally gifted at keeping you both within the time you have agreed upon. While timing does not have to be rigid or legalistic, you both will need time to share your experience. The gatekeeper keeps space open for this to happen.

Beginning Your Times Together

As you meet, remember that you both will need a few minutes to settle into this time and space together. As we come into any meeting, we bring whatever has been happening in our life during the day, week, or month. Some suggested ways of shifting into the quiet in the presence of God and each other are included in PART THREE under *Spiritual Disciplines.*

Being With: Listening and Responding

This is the time of making a space for the other person to walk into. We assist in creating that space by our willingness to lay aside our own agenda in order to listen with care and sensitivity to what our spiritual friend is sharing. Being truly present to our partner is harder at times than at others, especially if the events of our day or week have been especially stressful or energizing.

As the other person reads, speaks, or is sometimes silent, we will be listening for the way God is working, the way grace is happening, how the image of God is being formed in her.

We will also be listening for her response to God: Is it a response of resistance or a response of prayer and action? It is only as we ourselves become more aware of when we are opening our attention to God and when we are not, that we will become more able to notice this activity in our friend.

> It will not be a matter of trying to remember what some book said to do, and continuing a contrived "helpful" response. More and more you simply will be with the person as they need you to be with them. Your own experience in touching and glancing away from the same Reality with which your friend struggles gives you a common bond and sympathetic perception.[18]

As we listen, our underlying attitude is compassion. As we are aware of our own resistance and response to God and others, we are slower to correct or to tell our friend what he is to do. We become open and quiet in our listening and respond by saying what we observe, rather than trying to jump to conclusions.[19]

One of our natural tendencies is to want to solve problems. It is an expression of our desire to "help" the other person overcome or find some solution to their struggle. If we sense that our friend is not able to come to any resolution, we need to be aware of the helping responses that may arise within us. If we move into a "rescuer" or "parent" role, we will tend to take responsibility away from the other person and from God. A growing maturity will be evident as we allow the experience of the other to be open-ended and ongoing.

In spiritual friendship the shift is toward listening in the presence of God. If you are experiencing something of an impasse and no insight seems to come, you will find it helpful to turn to God and to wait in silence for a few minutes. This reflects an attitude of trust and dependency on God. We do not give birth to the answer for our friend. Rather, we are the midwife, waiting, assisting the process of giving birth to God's transforming presence in the other.

Sharing Your Experience

The basic content of what you share with your friend can grow out of your response to your reflection on the following questions. One question may stand out more than another for you. Do not feel that you need to slavishly work through the list each time you meet. The questions are designed only to help you become aware of movement in your spiritual journey:

What is my prayer experience like?
What happens when I pray or meditate on scripture?
What areas of my life is God touching?
How am I experiencing God's grace?
What is God like for me—in scripture, in times of prayer, or other times?
How have I cooperated with God this week (month)?
What am I not bringing openly before God? (e.g., anger, fear. . . .)
Where have I missed experiencing God's grace or love?
What do I need to confess?
What is changing within me as I listen to God?
What attitudes am I experiencing as I relate to others in my life?

In order to discover more clearly where you are in your prayer life, you may find it helpful to read sections from your journal (see page 48) to your friend (those sections you feel comfortable sharing). While journaling is easier for some to do than others, it is a helpful way to put out in front of you—in writing, doodling, or simple drawings and shapes—what you sense is going on in your spiritual life.

Bringing Closure

At the end of your time together, you may choose to pray for each other. You may want to mention those items your friend has asked to be held accountable for in the intervening time.

Accountability

As we sift through the various parts of our lives, we discover those areas where we feel God is asking us to change. One woman requests that her spiritual friend ask about her response to her thirteen-year-old daughter and to pray for her as she seeks to respond in love and wisdom. Another woman asks to be held accountable for her care of her own body, especially in the area of exercise. Still another person asks to be held accountable for his use of time as he seeks a healthy balance between work, relaxation, and prayerful solitude. Whatever the request, it is a sign of where the life of the Spirit is becoming incarnate, where the kingdom of God is showing up in our lives. The intent is not one of harsh judgment but rather of making known where we are seeking to move in harmony with the spirit of God within us.

We agree to be held accountable as we are ready. The focus of a small group, of which I was a member, was spiritual growth and mutual support. It took time for a deep sense of trust and openness to form, and some of us did not feel ready to be held accountable for a specific area of growth or action for over a year. The readiness of one or two seemed to help others consider where they could also be accountable, but the movement of God in one should never be used as coercion or manipulation of the other.

PART THREE

Being Receptive and Responsive to God

[..]

Chapter 8

Beginning the Conversation with God

[··]

Listen! I am standing at the door, knocking; if you hear my voice and open the door, I will come in to you and eat with you, and you with me. —*Revelation 3:20*

"No one really taught me that prayer was talking to God, but as I watched and listened to others praying, I assumed that was what prayer was."

"I learned to pray in church. We prayed prayers out of the prayer book."

"My mother prayed with me at bedtime; usually a set prayer, like 'Now I lay me down to sleep.' But sometimes she prayed other prayers. I remember asking her to pray for my dog Trusty when I was about eight. Trusty had been injured."

"I remember hearing my father pray in his study late at night, after most of us had gone to bed. I was so touched when I heard him mention me by name."

There were about eighteen of us sitting in a circle, exploring our earliest memories of prayer and how we had learned to pray. As I listened, I thought about my own journey.

I learned to pray by listening to others: a Sunday school teacher, a pastor, a youth group leader. For years I assumed that prayer was talking to God; bringing my requests, praises, concerns, confessions, and thanksgivings to God.

Like others in the circle, I saw myself taking the initiative to begin the conversation. But I had also seen the conversation as rather one-sided: persons who pray are doing the communicating while God is doing the listening. God's response would not be expected in the form of a dialogue or in the experience of God's presence. If God responded to the prayer, then the request made would be granted. God could also decide not to grant the request, but in either case, God was seen as conversing with us through actions. This view of prayer tends to lead us into a one-way street. When we do all the talking, we are deciding how far we will walk along this street and what we will include in our baggage as we travel. We usually carry no more than what we feel safe revealing to God.

> Many people with an interest in religion have been traumatized by life and perhaps by false or inaccurate teachings about God. Their image of God is such that all they want is to keep on his right side or to keep as far away from God as possible.[20]

When our image of who God is has been marred by persons and events in our past, we will feel more comfortable keeping God at a distance, whether we are aware of our fear of God or not. If we add the guilt we feel because of our own sinfulness, we have another compelling reason for avoiding intimacy with God. It helps us to recall what Peter said, after a flash of realization as to who Jesus was, "Go away from me, Lord, for I am a sinful man!" It also helps to recall that Jesus comforted him and calmed his fears.[21]

It is Jesus who calms our fears concerning God. When Philip expressed his longing to see God, he voiced the longing that has hovered in all of our hearts down through the centuries: "Lord, show us the Father, and we will be satisfied." Jesus consoled him by pointing to himself: "Whoever has seen me has seen the Father."[22] Jesus came to make peace, to heal the rift, to help us know God for who God truly is—the God who is love.

It is this loving God who shows up in all kinds of ways and begins a conversation with us. As we pause to reflect on the biblical story, we become aware that God initiates the relationships with Adam, with Abraham, with Samuel, with Moses, and with the children of Israel. In Jesus, God begins a conversation with us. John the apostle recognized God's initiative and wrote: "In this is love, not that we loved God but that he loved us and sent his Son."[23] Matthew begins and ends his Gospel in the awareness of the presence of God in Jesus Christ: "Name him Emmanuel, which means, 'God is with us,'" and "Remember, I am with you always, to the end of the age."[24] For the Gospel writers, this presence of God with us in Jesus Christ is at the core of the good news.

CHAPTER 9

Spiritual Disciplines

[··]

Spiritual disciplines can assist us in our becoming receptive to God's presence and in our response to the God who is always present to us.

Although we may feel uneasy when we hear the word *discipline,* we may be surprised at how many disciplines we use in a day in order to eat, travel, work, speak, and play. We are so used to measuring the coffee; we forget the discipline of learning how to use a measure. We hardly can remember learning the disciplines of counting and reading, although we read and use numbers every day. These disciplines are so much a part of us that we do not think of them as being difficult or getting in the way. Being able to read and count helps us to get where we need to go. And spiritual disciplines assist us in our receptivity to God. They are a way into God's presence.

Many of us tend to think that spiritual disciplines are something out of our reach, something more suited for priests or saints.

> Far from it. God intends the Disciplines of the spiritual life to be for ordinary human beings: people who have jobs, who care for children, who wash dishes and mow lawns.[25]

Just as we learned to read as children—a discipline that opens up our world to new discovery—so as children of God the spiritual disciplines open the way for us to discover God.

> God has given us the Disciplines of the spiritual life as a means of receiving his grace. The Disciplines allow us to place ourselves before God so that he can transform us.[26]

Spiritual disciplines are not a system of working our way to heaven. Rather, they are pathways into the presence of God. Just as maps give us some guidance as we travel, so spiritual disciplines are not the journey itself but assist us in our being present to God.

> Through the indwelling Spirit the human spirit is brought into immediate contact with higher spiritual reality. It looks upon, tastes, feels and sees the powers of the world to come and has a conscious encounter with God invisible . . . . Maybe Christ said all this more simply in John 14:21: "I . . . will manifest myself to him."[27]

The spiritual disciplines described below are to assist you as you enter into the Gospel of Matthew, walk with other disciples gathered around Jesus, and encounter Jesus for yourself. In addition, just as Matthew pays attention in his Gospel to the many different occasions and places where

God is present, use of the prayer disciplines will help you become aware of God's presence within yourself and in the world around you. This awareness is both comforting and transforming. "It is by being awake to this God in us that we can see him in the world around us."[28]

This being awake to God in all of life can happen as we enter into the life rhythm of the early disciples. We tend to emphasize the going and serving. Jesus invites us to shift our gaze and to pay attention to:

Coming
"(Jesus) went up the mountain and called to him those whom he wanted, and they came to him . . .

Being With
to be with him . . .

Responding
and to be sent out. . . ."[29]

CHAPTER 10

Disciplines to Assist Our Coming

[··]

We tend to live our lives in a state of fragmentation, thinking about one thing while doing another. We make plans for tomorrow while listening to another person talk. But just as those first disciples left their everyday tasks to be with Jesus, so Jesus calls us to walk away from the many voices and tasks that captivate our attention and energy in order to open our attention to God.

These little disciplines of *Coming* help us to re-collect all the fragments of our body, mind, and spirit and to be still, open, and receptive in the presence of God. Not all the prayer forms will work for all persons at all times. Experiment and see which disciplines help you open yourself to God.

Choosing a Place

Throughout the Gospels, it is reported that Jesus developed a rhythm of retreat for prayer and solitude. He walked away from the towns, cities, and people to be alone in the hills, the mountains, or on the lake. Often his disciples went with him. When they asked Jesus to teach them how to pray, he mentioned among other things, the need for retreat and solitude. "Whenever you pray, go into your room and shut the door and pray."[30]

Choosing a place to pray in our home assists us on many levels. It may only be a certain chair, but when we sit in that chair our intent is to be open to God and to place ourselves in God's presence. What else we introduce into that place can be those things that assist our being present for God.

Prayer Forms

After entering that place for prayer, using one of the following prayer forms will assist you to come more fully into God's presence.

1. As you come into the quiet place of your choosing, sit, kneel, or lie comfortably and still. Take some deep, slow breaths, breathing in and out very slowly. Feel your body relaxing. As you continue to breathe in and out slowly, allow your breathing out to be a movement of your letting go all that is blocking God and your breathing in the receiving of all that is from God.[31]

2. Light a candle in your prayer place. Sit in the quiet, allowing the stillness and the light of the candle to draw your attention into the quiet. Allow the candle to be a symbol of the light of God's presence.

3. Play some music that draws your attention toward stillness. As you listen, feel your body and mind slowing down and entering into quietness .

4. Stand with your feet slightly apart and your arms outstretched at either side of you. Move your arms slowly so that they are finally in front of you and your hands together. As you move your arms, reflect on the gathering of all of the pieces and events of your life and experience; and as your hands come together, offer them all to God.

5. After finding a comfortable place to sit, kneel, or lie, imagine yourself walking away from your daily surroundings and into the fields and hills where Jesus went to pray. Jesus is waiting for you there. As you come into his presence, notice what you bring with you. Whatever you bring may become the starting point of your dialogue with Jesus. Be sure that Jesus meets us where we are, not where we wish we could be. Once the "front burner" agenda is recognized and given its proper attention, then we are more open and receptive to reading and meditating on the scripture.

Sometimes the dialogue that develops as we set down our baggage in Jesus' presence becomes the focus and content of our time in the quiet. Like the psalmist we are praying out of our experience, and we may wish to write our own psalm in our journal or to record what was significant to us in this meeting with Jesus.[32]

CHAPTER 11

Disciplines to Assist Our Being With

[··]

In the Gospel of Matthew we are invited by Jesus to take an inward journey. Matthew had taken this journey for himself and recounts for us Jesus' call to "enter through the narrow gate" onto the hard road "that leads to life."[33]

A few disciplines are included here to assist us on that inner journey and in our reading of Matthew's Gospel. As we move through the Gospel, other spiritual disciplines will be introduced by Jesus for us to learn and do along with his disciples. Doing these disciplines with a spiritual friend or a small group can encourage our commitment and help us know that we are not alone on the road that Jesus says few travel.

Praying the Scriptures: Meditation and Contemplation

> What happens in meditation is that we create the emotional and spiritual space which allows Christ to construct an inner sanctuary in the heart. The wonderful verse "I stand at the door and knock . . . " was originally penned for believers, not unbelievers (Rev. 3:20) . . . . Meditation opens the door and although we are engaging in specific meditation exercises at specific times, the aim is to bring this living reality into all of life . . . . all we are and do.[34]

The Benedictines of the fifth century prayed with the scriptures in a form known as *lectio divina* (meaning sacred reading). Their desire was to integrate their life of prayer and work, and they refined this prayer form that actually had been used already for many years by other Christians. As practiced by the Benedictines, these are the steps involved in *lectio divina*.

There is a sense in which we come to the scriptures as if we were about to eat a meal we enjoy. Enjoy their flavor; savor their goodness as you would enjoy a favorite food. *Read the chosen passage slowly several times*, aloud if desired, allowing the words and phrases to linger within you as you read.

Stay with the words or phrases that catch your attention. Repeat them, turn them around in your mind, *chew* on them, if you will. Just as the food we eat begins to be digested and absorbed into our body, taking energy and nourishment to every cell in every place, so meditation allows the scripture to be absorbed into all corners of our life and being.

Allow your prayers—of confession, thanksgiving, petition, worship—*to form out of your meditation.*

Finally, *rest in the presence of God*. Wait quietly and simply be present to God for ten to fifteen minutes. Various thoughts will intrude into the quiet space. Simply allow them to be, and rather than focusing your attention on them, simply return your attention to God. At the end of this time in the quiet, give a simple prayer of thanks.

[··]

Another helpful way of meditating on events and poetry in the scriptures comes to us from the spiritual guidance of Ignatius of Loyola.[35]

Walk into the scene or story in the scripture and use all of your five senses to experience the event as if you were there: Rub your hands in the sand as you sit on the beach. Smell the fish the disciples catch. Feel the warmth of the sun on your back. Hear the conversations between Jesus and those gathered around him. Taste the bread and fish given by Jesus to the hungry crowd. You can find yourself becoming part of the story, not just as an onlooker but as an active participant.

> Resist the temptation to pass over many passages superficially. Our rushing reflects our internal state and our internal is what needs to be transformed . . . . take a single event, . . . or a few verses, . . . and allow it to take root in you. Seek to live the experience.[36]

When you *begin to move beyond your imagination*, you begin to encounter Jesus, and you discover that you are encountered by him.

Respond to Jesus in prayer—confession, thanksgiving, petition, and praise.

Then simply allow the picture to fade and *be present to Jesus in the quiet* for ten or fifteen minutes. If your mind wanders, simply return your attention gently to Jesus. At the end of your time in the quiet give a simple prayer of thanks.

Journaling

Some of us like to write, others of us are less comfortable recording experiences in words on paper. However, some kind of written, sketched, or doodled reflection is helpful. It can help us begin to see on the page what is happening within.

> When we commit our observations to writing we are taking what is inside us and placing it outside us. We are holding a piece of our life in our hands where we can look at it, and meditate on it, and deepen our understanding of it.
> Beginning our work of observation by discerning our tendency to lie develops our capacity for openness and honesty, puts us in touch with our real self, and helps that self to make the movement toward becoming God's word in the world.[37]

Journaling can also be a way to converse with God by writing a prayer or a letter to God, or by writing a conversation with Jesus and "listening" with our pencil as Jesus responds.

Some persons like a loose-leaf notebook; others prefer the spiral kind. Purchasing a notebook that suits your preference is one way of saying that you are paying attention to your spiritual journey. The content of your meeting with your spiritual friend can come from what you feel comfortable sharing from journal entries.

As you journal, do not be concerned about spelling or how the words or sketches or whatever you choose to express comes out on the paper. This journal is for you. It is a record of your inner journey and can help you discover patterns, needs, blocks, and growth.

CHAPTER 12

Disciplines to Assist Our Responding

[··]

Prayer Focus

At the beginning of each week's reading guide, a short prayer is included. It is one sentence to carry with you each day throughout that week. Brief prayers such as these help us to open our attention to God.

Recollection

This is a helpful discipline to carry with us through the day. The older name, *consciousness examen*, means that we become aware. We ask the spirit of God to help us see our day as the spirit of Jesus sees our day.

A simple way to begin is to ask ourselves:

How have I been aware of God today?
Where have I missed God today?

Where have I moved with God today?
Where have I blocked God's movement today?

For each week of readings, some further suggestions are given to guide your reflection on the scriptures and the issues that are being raised on your journey. These questions for reflection are also a form of *consciousness examen*. You will find them in each daily reading section.

PART FOUR

A Reading Guide in the Gospel of Matthew

[··]

CHAPTER 13

Introduction to the Reading Guide

[··]

You are invited into Matthew's Gospel and world.

Matthew reveals little direct information about himself, only that he was a tax collector before he was called by Jesus to follow him. However, this little piece of autobiography is revealing. On the one hand, Matthew's occupation as a representative of the Roman government that occupied Palestine lowered his standing in Jewish opinion polls: to the patriotic Jew, Matthew was a traitor; to the scribes and Pharisees who had developed their own equivalent of a religious caste system, he was among the untouchables. On the other hand, his employment assured him of a sizable income and kept him in with those who were caught up with gaining influence and popularity and procuring the money needed to assure both.

When Matthew responds to Jesus' invitation, a deep and ongoing transformation begins. He no longer needs to find refuge in money and its illusive power to buy friendship. He becomes aware that God's kingdom is larger than the Roman state (that dominated much of the then-known world). As a Jew, he realizes that what God had begun with Abraham and Sarah—the giving of a promise, the birthing of a people in relationship with God—God was now moving to fulfill. God is on the move, the kingdom of God is here and coming, God is present to us in Jesus Christ until the end of the age.

However vast this picture may seem, Matthew's eyes are also opened to see God in the everyday. The religious leaders had manipulated the Law of Moses so that any righteousness and acceptability before God seemed attainable only by scrupulous attention and obedience to the Law and the traditions of the Jewish elders. They had squeezed any life out of the meaning and intent of the Law, and in so doing had created deep factions in society between who was acceptable in their sight—the "righteous"—and who was a sinner and literally untouchable. As he continues to be with Jesus, to pay attention to what Jesus says and does, Matthew is deeply aware of a greater righteousness—the loving and merciful presence of God in Jesus, bringing the kingdom of God. This greater righteousness moves beyond the barbed-wire boundaries of the religious leaders and flows with mercy into the lives of people—healing the sick and mentally ill; freeing the demon-oppressed; embracing the untouchable lepers and tax collectors; empowering women; paying special attention to children, for their way of being and seeing is how we enter the kingdom; bringing justice and blessing to the poor; and congratulating those who are not Jews for their faith in Jesus.

Matthew learns to pay attention to where God is moving in people's lives—through dreams, angelic visitors, boat trips, a boy's lunch, little children who want to be touched and held, conversations about washing hands, wine and broken bread, the cross; and above all, through Jesus himself.

The spiritual discipline of meditative reading of the scriptures using *lectio divina* or the Ignatian approach of walking into the story will enable you to be present to where God is moving, both in Matthew's Gospel and in the everyday world of your own life.

Arrangement of Readings

The readings move slowly through the Gospel, allowing time for stopping to visit and reflect. Although reading the Bible through in one year is a commendable discipline and gives a helpful overview of the scriptures, such an approach can also be like trying to eat a five-course meal in a few minutes. Meditative reading takes small bites, enjoys the flavors, and allows the spiritual food to be assimilated into all corners of our life.

To help you slow down and come into the scriptures in an open and attentive way, a prayer of COMING is suggested. In the time of BEING WITH, five readings are included for each week, with suggestions for reflection and simply being attentive to Jesus. On the sixth day some thoughts are given to assist you in your reflection on the week and to what you might like to share with your spiritual friend when you have your time together. A short PRAYER FOCUS is included in each week's reading guide for you to travel with each day that week.

Do not be legalistic as you read, reflect, and journal. We have a tendency to judge ourselves if we do not complete everything every day. If you miss a day's reading, or even several days', simply acknowledge that and move on. If you are only able to commit yourself to some time in the quiet two, three, or four days a week, accept where you are for now.

God with Us on All Our Journeys

[··]

PRAYER FOCUS

Lord, help me to open my attention to your presence.

COMING

Before you turn to the scripture for the day, settle your body, mind, and spirit in the quiet. You may find that one of the COMING exercises in PART THREE is helpful .

BEING WITH

Turn to the scripture for the day and listen to God's word in a slow, thoughtful way. You may want to read the text aloud several times. Then, think through the questions and place yourself in the story. Simply be present; notice who is there and what they are doing. What is God doing and saying? How are persons responding to what God is doing and saying? How does it affect others? Who do you identify with? In what way is God present to you? How do you feel after this time of meditation? What shift has occurred in you, and where is it taking you?

[DAY 1]
God's care throughout all generations
GENESIS 12:1-5; MATTHEW 1:1-6, 16-17

Almost two thousand years are spanned by this genealogy. As Abraham and Sarah heard God's call to leave their country and their people to go to a land that God would show them, how little they knew of God's purpose! But they listened to God and began the journey. They discovered that it was a journey of trust and receiving, of believing God and opening themselves to receive the promise, blessing, and presence of God.

Over the years many other men and women became carriers of the promise and the blessing. Matthew lists some of them for us (Matthew 1:1-17); each one continues the journey begun by Abraham and Sarah, carrying the promise as they walked, stumbled, and sometimes fell. But God was at work down through the years, coming to them, being present, keeping the promise to bring the Savior into the world. In Jesus all of us are blessed.

As you continue this time of BEING WITH, remember that you are also beginning a journey, a journey of trust and receiving, of opening yourself to God and what God brings to you. You will also be journeying with a spiritual friend, sharing your experience and listening to his or her experience. You may want to review the instructions for meditation and contemplation in PART THREE as you walk into the Genesis story and begin your own journey.

Journaling is a helpful way to record in a few words what we experience in our times with God. This week you are also invited to write a brief account of your life to share with your spiritual friend during your first time together. Suggestions will be given each day for what you might want to include. Today begin your account of your own beginnings by recording those significant people and events in your past before you were born. You may have heard family members speak of these.

[DAY 2]
Emmanuel: God with us
MATTHEW 1:18-25

Mary was pregnant but was not yet Joseph's wife—a scandal in the eyes of the town. Joseph was a good man; yet manipulated by fear, Joseph decided to leave her (quietly) to carry the unborn alone. Then his sleep is shattered by the truth. The scandal was Emmanuel: God with us! Moved by God, Joseph opened himself to the risk of being a receiver of the promised blessing. He took Mary within his embrace and with her the Christ-child, Jesus. What are the two names given to the baby and their meanings? (vv. 21, 23) How do the names speak of who God is for you?

Continue BEING WITH as you are present to God in quiet attentiveness. After this time of waiting, you may want to bring other persons or concerns to God in prayers of intercession.

In your journaling, continue your reflection on your past by recording some of the stories surrounding your birth. Who named you? What do you know about your name(s)?

[DAY 3]
Gifts for the journey
MATTHEW 2:1-12

Reflect on these responses to Jesus' birth: Herod (v. 3) and the wise men (vv. 2, 10-11). How is God protecting the child Jesus here? (v. 12)

Walk into the story—listen, touch, smell, worship. Some persons find they encounter God as they begin journaling their experience of the scriptures and their inner responses to God. Conclude your time with God with intercession for your family, friends, church, and world.

As you continue to reflect on your own beginning, add to your story the names of significant persons in your early childhood. Why were they important to you? What kinds of "gifts" did they bring into your life?

[DAY 4]
God's protection means becoming refugees.
MATTHEW 2:13-18

We are confronted with a tragedy and gross injustice here: the misuse of power in the hands of Herod, who represents the state. Here we see one of the faces of evil as it seeks to destroy God's plan in bringing Jesus to be "God with us." But behind the scenes and in the midst of danger, we find God, protecting this family. Jesus and his parents become refugees in Egypt, even as God's grace is present to grieving parents in Bethlehem.

Enter the story; reflect as you are present and listen. After a time of quiet presence, conclude your time with prayers of intercession for family, friends, church, and world. Possibly other instances of injustice will come to mind; bring these persons and their needs into God's presence.

As you add to your life account, report on the important events in your life: the times of great change, of great sadness, of great joy. What meaning do these events have for you?

[DAY 5]
God has a place.
MATTHEW 2:19-23

For Mary and Joseph this is a time of looking for a place to live, to raise Jesus. How do they depend on God for direction?

God shows up in Joseph's life in dreams (1:20; 2:13, 22). Spend some time walking into the story and being present with Mary, Joseph, and the baby. Listen to Joseph's dreams and notice the various ways God shows up in people's lives. Conclude with prayers for your family, friends, church, and world.

Complete your account of your beginnings by remembering the places you have lived (houses, towns, cities, countries). How have these places served to shape who you are today?

[DAY 6]
Responding through Reflection
The sixth day of each week is a day to reflect on your journey of the first five days. You may want to come into God's presence as you do regularly.

Once you are still and centered, thank God for helping you become aware of God's presence this week. Now read over your journal entries. Select a day on which you were most deeply aware of God's presence in your life. Bring this entry with you into the presence of God. In what ways does this insight/learning affect your life? What is your response to God? to others?

Preparing for Your Time Together
Collect the pieces of your autobiography to give to your spiritual friend during your time together. Reflect on which part of your journaling you would be comfortable sharing.

You may want to reread the chapter on *Your Times Together* in preparation for the meeting with your spiritual friend.

God Comes to Us in Jesus

[··]

PRAYER FOCUS
Lord, help me to open my attention to your presence.

COMING
Before you turn to the scripture for the day, bring all of yourself into the presence of God. You may want to use one of the exercises from PART THREE.

BEING WITH
After you turn to the scripture for the day, listen to God's word in a slow, thoughtful way. You may want to read the text aloud several times. After you have read the text, reflect on the questions, and then move into the story. Place yourself in the scene, noticing who is there, what they are doing, where they are. What is God doing? How are persons responding to

God? to each other? Who do you find yourself identifying with? What is your response to God?

[DAY 1]
Prepare for his coming.
MATTHEW 3:1-12

As you read through Matthew's Gospel during the next eleven weeks, you will be invited to sit and to walk with all kinds of people. They are people who are searching and waiting, people who do not always know what they need. As God comes to them in Jesus, their responses are mixed.

Where do you find yourself today? Who do you meet there? How does John the Baptist envision the work of Jesus? List the tasks that John expects Jesus to do (3:10-12).

What response to God's messenger, John, do you see and hear in people's lives? What response do you feel and hear within yourself?

This week, reflect on the times when you became aware of God's encountering you. You may want to write an account in one sitting to share with your spiritual friend or to write a little each day as you follow the daily readings.

Reflect on this question for today: Who are the persons who influenced your spiritual journey and your beginning responses to God?

[DAY 2]
Being receptive to his coming
MATTHEW 3:13-17

Now Jesus comes. Sit quietly and notice how he comes: receiving from John and receiving from God the Spirit and God the Father. Jesus is open to receiving how God brings God's gracious presence into this world. John is surprised. How Jesus comes to him is not what John expected. Throughout Matthew we will see this gap between what people expected the Messiah to be like and what Jesus actually is like. The same is true in our own experience. Our journey is to discover what God is really like.

> Thou shalt know him when he comes,
> not by the din of drums,
> not by the vantage of his airs,
> nor by anything he wears;
> neither by his crown, nor his gown.
> For his presence known shall be
> by the holy harmony
> which his coming makes in thee.[38]

As you look back over your life's journey, record the God-moments in your life; those times when God seemed near and touched your life in some way.

[DAY 3]
Jesus begins his ministry in silence and solitude.
MATTHEW 4:1-11

Now Jesus is led by the Spirit into the wilderness. Follow him as he leaves the crowds gathered around John in the Jordan River valley and hikes up the hilly slopes to spend time in the quiet of the wilderness.

He has been sent by God to save the world. How will he do it? What vision of ministry will Jesus develop in this time alone in retreat?

Satan presents several possibilities:

1. To use his power to provide for his own physical needs and, in so doing, lose sight of the deeper, spiritual needs that only God can satisfy (v. 4). The focus here is not on denying our need for food but on denying our spiritual hungers and longings in our grasping for food. Jesus addresses this again in 6:25ff.

2. To perform the spectacular and use God to bail him out of any risk in order to get people's attention and thus

prove God's presence (vv. 6-7). Jesus refuses to manipulate persons or God.

3. To win the allegiance of the kingdoms of the world by worshiping Satan (vv. 8-10). The lure of all that the world has to offer is dangled before Jesus.

Satan tests us in those places where we are most vulnerable. Jesus' place of testing had to do with his identity as God's son (vv. 3, 6) and how he would do the work God had commissioned him to do. It is in the quiet of solitude that Jesus discerns the lies and deceptions being suggested to him. He leans on the scriptures for guidance and for his responses to Satan.

Reflect on any "desert times" you may have experienced—times of silence, aloneness, or testing—times when God seemed distant.

Where did you find strength and help during those times?

[DAY 4]
Jesus is light, shining in our darkness.
MATTHEW 4:12-17

As you reflect on the places mentioned and on the prophecy of Isaiah that Matthew quotes (vv. 14-16), what images come into your mind? Now place yourself beside the lake and watch Jesus coming (vv. 12-13). What do you see and hear as Jesus begins to preach (v. 17)? Now what does the fulfillment of Isaiah's prophecy look and sound like? In what way is this a God-moment for the people in Galilee? for you?

As you continue to trace your spiritual journey, reflect on how you have come to enter into the kind and gracious rule of God's kingdom. How has Jesus encountered you? What has been your response to him?

[DAY 5]
Leaving our nets to follow and be with Jesus
MATTHEW 4:18-22

You are still on the beach beside the lake. What group of people do you meet? What does Jesus ask of them? What does it cost them to follow him?

What kind of God-moment is this for Peter, Andrew, James, and John? for the parents and families they left behind (v. 22)? for you?

As you continue to reflect on your spiritual journey, think today about how you are becoming a disciple of Jesus. What have you left behind? Add these reflections to your account to share with your spiritual friend.

[DAY 6]
Responding through Reflection

This is a day to reflect on your journey for this week. Once you are still and centered, reflect on the times you have been aware of God this week. Now read over your journal entries, selecting an entry you would like to spend more time with. Bring this entry with you into the presence of God. How does this entry reveal God's gracious presence and work in you? What is your response to God?

Preparing for Your Time Together

Bring the written accounts of your spiritual journey together to share with your spiritual friend during your time together. Reflect on which part of your other journaling you would feel comfortable sharing.

Listening to Jesus

[··]

PRAYER FOCUS
Lord, help me to listen to you.

COMING
This week you are invited to join other followers of Jesus as they sit on the mountainside and listen to him. Before you turn to the scripture each day, find a comfortable place to sit and settle your body, mind, and spirit in the quiet of the mountain slope and the presence of Jesus.

BEING WITH
After you turn to the scripture for the day, listen to God's word in a slow, thoughtful way, reading the text aloud if you like.

This week, since the readings (after DAY 1) are teachings of Jesus rather than story, read the text until you come to a word or a phrase that attracts your attention. Stop and reread the phrase, savoring its goodness and nourishment. Read over *Praying the Scriptures* in CHAPTER 11 to help you allow the word of God into your heart.

We do not come to be with Jesus because we are righteous or strong. The people gathered around Jesus because they were needy. In his sermon Jesus begins to explain the profound difference between the religious leaders' teaching about attaining righteousness through their interpretation of the Law and traditions and the greater righteousness that moves beyond the Law to a relationship with God in Jesus Christ.

Our sinful, restricted self is uncomfortable and fights being revealed. But deeper within us is the longing for God, placed within our true self by God. We come to God as we are: caught by sin and longing for God; and we are always met by God's grace and mercy.

[DAY 1]
Sitting with those who gather to be with Jesus
MATTHEW 4:23–5:1

List the kinds of persons who gather around Jesus (4:24; 5:1). What is going on within you as you sit alongside them? Who are you in the crowd? Where are you sitting? Why did you choose to sit there? What is your experience of Jesus just now? of God?

[DAY 2]
Jesus meets us where we find ourselves
lacking and longing.
MATTHEW 5:2-12

Much of our world's noise and activity seems designed to silence the hungers and longings of our heart. Maybe we are unaware of these deep, inner hungers. They are there, but perhaps no one has encouraged us to pay attention. Jesus speaks to the hungers of our heart, to our inner longings.

If we listen to Jesus, we will discover that these longings are the doorways through which we come to God and through which God comes to us. Jesus says that the people with these longings are "blessed"—are welcomed into God's family, are brought into God's kind and gracious presence, are connected to one another.

You may want to make a list of heart longings found in verses 3-11. Which ones do you find within yourself?

Bring those longings into your presence for God today.

[DAY 3]
Healing presence rather than blind form
MATTHEW 5:13-20

Salt enhances flavor; it preserves and cleanses. Light helps us see and brings us and others to recognize God (v. 16). (Remember that Jesus is God's light coming.)

Throughout the Gospel of Matthew, Jesus and his followers will be criticized by the Pharisees and teachers of the Law. These religious party members were convinced that by their practice of the *outward* forms of religious tradition and of the Law, they became righteous in the eyes of God. They avoided any awareness of their *inward* needs and longings or the inward longings of others.

Jesus calls his followers to a greater righteousness—or faithfulness as *Today's English Version* translates it. He calls them to a righteousness of the heart. The laws of the Old Testament were given to guide God's people in their understanding of what God requires, but over the years the people moved toward maintaining the outward form and missed the true heart intent. Jesus says he has come to make the teaching of the law "come true" (v. 17, TEV).

In the following readings from the Sermon on the Mount and in Jesus' teachings throughout Matthew, we will discover what he means by those words and begin to see what the greater righteousness—greater faithfulness— looks like. What God requires of us and what the society around us values are usually two very different things!

[DAY 4]
Faces of our needy self: anger and how we express it
MATTHEW 5:21-26

We have no problem agreeing that murder is wrong. But Jesus goes deeper, touching on the attitudes and motives of our needy self.

The call to a greater righteousness and faithfulness requires us to probe within. When do I become angry? How do I express my anger? by attacking and insulting others (v. 22)?

As we open ourselves to God (v. 23), we become aware of the hostile attitudes we carry within ourselves toward others. Rather than covering up our hostility, Jesus calls us to make peace, to be reconciled. As we listen to God, we become more attentive to what is within.

[DAY 5]
Faces of our needy self: revenge and hate
MATTHEW 5:38-48

The greater faithfulness to which Jesus is calling us is not to keep a list of laws. We are coming into a family—God's family. The greater righteousness and faithfulness is to live in relationship with God and with one another.

How does Jesus call us to pay someone back (vv. 38-42)? How does Jesus call us to respond to our enemy (vv. 43-44)?

As we learn such responses, we are showing a family resemblance (v. 45)!

Bring any struggle you discover within yourself into your presence for God.

[DAY 6]
Responding through Reflection

As you look back over the week, reflect on how God has been at work in your life. As you listen, what do you hear God saying to you? What is your response? In what ways may you have blocked God's voice? Where do you need to experience God's grace and forgiveness? Where are you still struggling?

Preparing for Your Time Together

As you come together, be attentive to each other, listen with openness and compassion. Share with each other how God has been at work in your life this week and how you have responded.

What commitments are you making and sharing with each other? For what do you choose to be held accountable until you meet next time?

Listening to Jesus Teach about Spiritual Disciplines

[··]

PRAYER FOCUS
Lord, help me to be present for you.

COMING
Before you turn to the scripture for the day, settle your body, mind, and spirit in the quiet. You may find one of the exercises in PART THREE helpful to you.

BEING WITH
Turn to the scripture and listen to God's word in a slow, thoughtful way. The comments and questions for each day may help in your reflection.

Place yourself on the grass near Jesus and listen to him speak about spiritual disciplines. He invites you to an inward journey and describes some of the pathways into God's presence on the journey. Journal your insights.

[DAY 1]
Giving to the needy
MATTHEW 6:1-4

Jesus begins with an outward discipline: helping the needy. However, he asks us to go on an inward journey, to reflect on our inner motives as we serve God in this way. The first stopping place on this journey inward is to discover who controls us: Is it God, or is it the people around us and what they think of what we do (6:1)? The task for us is to keep listening to God in the quiet.

We may pull back from the enormous need within the world, wondering what one person can do. Jesus simply asks us to give, to be attentive to the needs of others, and to be attentive to God who is present as we give. Such listening to God opens our attention to the greater reality of the world of God's spirit and presence, and we find ourselves gradually becoming unhooked from the control of the world's values.

[DAY 2]
Prayer
MATTHEW 6:5-15

Jesus withdrew from being with people in order to pray (Matthew 14:22-23; Mark 1:35), and he invites us to follow him into the presence of God. When we do, we are once again moving into the world of the unseen, the greater reality in which Jesus lives and moves. To become aware of this freeing reality, Jesus instructs us to retreat, to find a private place for prayer.

While we can pray anywhere at any time, Jesus still calls us to shut out the world's insistent beckonings by choosing special places and times for prayer. As you reflect on this passage, think about where you go to pray.

He then teaches a prayer that helps us understand a little of what the greater reality of God's kingdom is about. You may find it helpful to pray this prayer slowly and reflectively and then to journal your insights.

[DAY 3]
Fasting
MATTHEW 6:16-18

While Jesus does not make fasting a commandment, he does include fasting in his teachings about spiritual disciplines. Our devotion to God is to be the central motive of our fasting.

> Fasting must forever center on God. It must be God-initiated and God-ordained. Like the prophetess Anna, we need to be "worshiping with fasting" (Luke 2:37). Every other purpose must be subservient to God . . . . More than any other Discipline, fasting reveals the things that control us. This is a wonderful benefit to the true disciple who longs to be transformed into the image of Jesus Christ. We cover up what is inside us with food and other good things, but in fasting these things surface.[39]

Besides abstaining from food, there are other ways of fasting: abstinence from television, overspending, or overworking, etc.

[DAY 4]
Contemplation
MATTHEW 6:19-34

If we are not worrying about what other people think, then we are often worrying about something else: money (vv.

19-24) or the things we need to live (vv. 25-34) or even life itself (v. 27).

Jesus gives us a simple but profound way to free ourselves from this kind of slavery and the worry that feeds it. He invites us to contemplation. As a first exercise, he instructs us to ponder carefully and prayerfully the birds and the flowers, both created and cared for by God.

Spend fifteen minutes in quiet awareness of the birds and flowers and trees. Simply be present to God and creation. Listen and be receptive to God's care and presence.

[DAY 5]
Discernment
MATTHEW 7:1-12

Jesus came to make the blind see (Matthew 11:5). He sees deep into our inner person and invites us to follow him as he lays his hands on those places where we hold on to attitudes and fears that distort how we see others and how we see God. This is the inner journey, the journey whose pathway is marked by the spiritual disciplines.

What is your heart's attitude toward people (vv. 3-4)? What is your heart's image of God as you pray (v. 11)?

[DAY 6]
Responding through Reflection
MATTHEW 7:13-14

Jesus describes the way to life: it is narrow, difficult, and lonely. We need the companionship of others on the road. Spiritual friendship lightens the journey, helping us to know we are among fellow pilgrims on the way.

As you reflect on the spiritual disciplines you have focused on this week, you may want to prayerfully choose one or two to continue using as you travel. Spend some time in those disciplines today.

Preparing for Your Time Together

After taking some time to come into the quiet together, share something from your inner journey with your friend. Listen for what God is saying and doing and how your friend is responding to God.

Share with each other the spiritual disciplines you are choosing to use. In the following times together, be listening for each other's experience and learning in your use of those disciplines.

Being with Jesus on the Outward Journey

[..]

PRAYER FOCUS
*Lord, help me to pay attention to your presence
in the people around me.*

COMING
As you come into a quiet place, still your mind and your body. Allow the rush and noise to die down. Choose your favorite exercise to assist you as you get in touch with your desire for God.

BEING WITH
This week, as you turn prayerfully to the scriptures, you will be walking with Jesus and the disciples away from the mountainside and into the streets and homes where people

live and work and wonder. In the outward journey, we begin living out what we have heard from God in the quiet.

[DAY 1]
Hearing and obeying
MATTHEW 7:24-27

As you read these words of Jesus, reflect on the two kinds of foundations. Ask God to help you see what foundations you have learned to build your life on.

What does your inner security have to do with hearing and obeying Jesus?

Remember that on the outward journey your sense of security will sometimes be tested.

[DAY 2]
Restoring the outcast
MATTHEW 8:1-4

Walk into the story today and be with Jesus as he moves toward the leper, welcomes his request, and reaches out to touch him. Notice also how Jesus makes sure this man is restored to community—an important part of his healing. (You may want to read Leviticus 14 to discover why Jesus told the man to go to his priest and offer a sacrifice.)

In what way do you need to be restored? As you come to Jesus at the bottom of the hill, what do you need to ask of him?

[DAY 3]
Affirming faith
MATTHEW 8:5-13

As Jesus walks into Capernaum he meets another "outcast" —a military officer in the Roman occupation army in Israel. Stand on the street in this town on the northern edge of Lake Galilee, and listen carefully to Jesus' reply to the man.

All through the Gospel of Matthew, we will be hearing Jesus respond and teach about faith. Faith *sees* God's greater reality and comes into the community of the kingdom of heaven (v. 11). As you walk with Jesus and your spiritual friend, your "little" reality will begin to crumble, so that the greater reality of God's kingdom can grow within you and around you.

What have you experienced of God's greater reality since you began walking with your spiritual friend?

[DAY 4]
Faith and priorities
MATTHEW 8:14-22; MARK 1:35-38

After you have read both passages, reflect on what it means to the disciples to follow Jesus. What concerns do the disciples have? Where does Jesus find his direction?

In the silence and solitude with God, Jesus is released from the many voices that clamor for his attention so that he can listen to the one voice of his heavenly Father. The spiritual disciplines of solitude and prayer free us to listen and obey (Matthew 7:24).

What are you hearing in the quiet?

[DAY 5]
Storm in the midst of obedience
MATTHEW 8:23-27

Today you are in the boat with Jesus and the other disciples, rowing toward Gadara, on the other side of Lake Galilee. In the midst of obedience, a fierce storm hits! The disciples' sense of security is threatened.

> The "sea" is a place of great peril and destruction: . . . and although Jesus has mastery over it, it evokes feelings of cowardice, fear, and little faith in the disciples.[40]

Speak to Jesus about your experience in the storm and the boat. What storms are you encountering in your own life? Bring these events into the presence of God also. Then wait and listen in the quiet.

Make a note of your prayer experience in your journal.

[DAY 6]
Responding through Reflection

As you look back over this week, reflect on when you have experienced God's presence and what you have heard God saying to you. What spiritual disciplines are helping you pay attention to God? What is your response to God today?

Preparing for Your Time Together

You will begin listening to each other's listening and obeying today. Share what you are hearing God say and how you are responding, not only within yourself, but also share the ways in which your inward journey is beginning to change your outward journey.

Still with Jesus on the Outward Journey

[··]

PRAYER FOCUS
Lord, help me to see as you see, to hear as you hear.

COMING
Take a few minutes to consciously place yourself in God's presence. Let go of the activity and pressures of the day and be still.

BEING WITH
This week you will continue walking with Jesus and waiting while he takes time to be present to people whom many others would rather avoid. You will also be present as people begin to criticize and reject Jesus.

Listen to Jesus. Listen to the rejection. Listen to your own inner feelings and thoughts as you encounter persons who are difficult to be with and persons who reject and criticize.

[DAY 1]
Responding to oppression and paralysis of spirit
MATTHEW 8:28–9:8

After the stormy ride, you are confronted by two men whose lives are full of storm and confusion. They live in a cemetery and no one dares to go near them. But Jesus is unafraid.

Jesus accepts the presence of demons as a present reality, rather than denying that they exist or refusing to respond to people who are oppressed by their presence. He listens to the demons screaming in fear at him and with calm authority orders the oppressive and controlling spirits to leave the men alone.

The people in the town ask Jesus to leave. Anyone casting out demons is a threat to them!

After returning to Capernaum, another man enters the story: a paralyzed man who is carried by friends to Jesus. As you are present in the story, watch and listen.

Who is present? What inner longings is Jesus aware of in the paralyzed man? What are the responses of those watching and listening? Which persons do you see living and moving into the greater reality of God's gracious rule, and which ones are stuck in their own self-righteousness?

What inner longings, debilitating oppressions, or needs for forgiveness do you want to bring to Jesus today? Journal your insights and learnings.

[DAY 2]
Calling the outcasts
MATTHEW 9:9-17

We continue walking with Jesus and the disciples through the streets of Capernaum. He invites Matthew to join him, a man who collected taxes from the Jews for the Roman occupation forces. He and many others were considered the untouchables in Jewish society. But Jesus lives in solidarity with Matthew and his friends as he sits and eats with them. Such solidarity brings criticism from the Pharisees.

In your meditation, listen to the responses within yourself. Who do you find it hard to be with? difficult to listen to? Journal your insights and listen for Jesus' speaking to you.

[DAY 3]
Being present to the grieving and the needy
MATTHEW 9:18-26

While you are walking with Jesus on the streets of Capernaum, two more persons with great need come to Jesus: a father whose daughter has just died and a woman who has been severely ill for twelve years. Jesus hears their prayers, both the spoken and the unspoken ones.

What is your response to the father? the woman? the crowds? Journal your insights and reflections.

[DAY 4]
Shouting for mercy
MATTHEW 9:27-34

Place yourself on the road again as two blind men begin to follow Jesus, shouting for mercy and believing that Jesus can heal them. As they leave the house where Jesus is staying, a man who cannot speak is brought in. Jesus restores sight to the blind and speech to the mute.

The crowd is amazed. The Pharisees condemn Jesus and begin to accuse him of being demon possessed.

What is your response to people who shout out their need in some way? Sit and talk with Jesus about your responses. Journal your insights.

[DAY 5]
Jesus invites you to respond
MATTHEW 9:35-38

Today you begin traveling with Jesus as he ministers in other towns and villages. As you stand and watch, listen closely. How does Jesus see the crowds (v. 36)? How does he ask you and his disciples to respond (v. 37-38)?

Journal your response to Jesus' request.

[DAY 6]
Responding through Reflection

As you come into this time of reflection, ask the Holy Spirit to help you see your week as God sees. Look over the events of the week. In what areas do you sense God's presence? Ask God to show you where God has been present in your life—with you or in others.

Take some time to reflect on your inner attitudes and feelings. Pay attention to your experiences of love, joy, harmony, freedom. Take note of any experiences of pain, confusion, anger, anxiety, or entrapment.

How is God speaking to you, drawing you, in these experiences? In what ways are you responding to or cooperating with God? In what ways are you not?

What is your prayer now? Is it confession, praise, thanksgiving, petition, intercession?

Preparing for Your Time Together

In your time together with your spiritual friend, take a few minutes to come into each other's presence and the presence of God.

Then share with each other how God has been present to you this week and how you are responding. Is there a place you sense the need to focus your attention on? a place to pray more about? or a place to take action on?

As you grow in trust and openness toward each other, you will be able to ask for each other's prayer support concerning specific areas of inner change, resistance, and growth.

Preparation for Your Outward Journey

[..]

*Lord, help me to trust you for all I need
on the outward journey.*

COMING

Jesus invites us to come, to be with him, and then to go out. In this time of coming to him, choose a prayer exercise that will help you to be still in body, mind, and spirit.

BEING WITH

Last week's readings concluded with Jesus' asking his disciples to pray that God would send out people to work in the field of his harvest.

Our concerns become our prayers. In prayer, we hear God. As we listen, we find a way to respond to the concerns God planted within us. This is all the movement of God's spirit within us. Praying and listening brings us into the place where God is moving.

[DAY 1]
We go without luggage.
MATTHEW 10:1-15

Jesus is teaching us deep lessons of trust and dependency. He tells his disciples to carry only what he has given them (vv. 7-10), to accept the hospitality of others (vv. 11-15), and to give what they have been given (vv. 8, 12, 19).

What kind of responses do you hear and feel within yourself as you reflect on what Jesus is saying?

[DAY 2]
We go in God's care.
MATTHEW 10:24-31

In the same way that persons respond to Jesus, so they respond to those who serve him (vv. 24-25). (See 9:34; 12:24.)

Instead of living within the constricted reality of those who reject and criticize, Jesus invites us to move within the larger reality of God's ability (v. 28), God's care (v. 29), and God's knowing (v. 30).

As members of God's family (v. 25), every detail of our need is known to God. Nothing escapes God's attention. Just at the time when we feel the most fearful, misunderstood, or rejected, we can remember that we live and move within the great reality. Jesus, once rejected and crucified, is with us now in solidarity.

Take some time in the quiet to speak to God about your fears, your needs. Journal your insights, learnings.

[Day 3]
We carry a cross.
Matthew 10:34-39

In the greater reality of God's kingdom, losing is gaining. That is made clear in these verses where Jesus tells us that he brings a sword (vv. 34-36) and those in which he tells us that we must carry a cross (vv. 37-39).

As we listen to the lessons for the outward journey, he asks us where our first love and loyalty lie. What does it mean to you to say "Lord Jesus"? Journal your insights.

[Day 4]
Jesus' solidarity with us
Matthew 10:40-42

Jesus identifies closely with those who follow and serve him (vv. 40-42). Spend time today waiting in Jesus' presence. You may find it helpful to visualize Jesus sitting among his disciples, teaching. Place yourself among the group. Wait and listen.

Journal your reflections.

[Day 5]
Return and rest.
Matthew 11:25-30

The disciples go out in obedience to Jesus' directions. After completing a time of ministry, they return. (See also Luke 9:1-6, 10.) They are both joyful and tired, and their faith and obedience bring joy to Jesus (vv. 25-27).

This is the rhythm of a life with Jesus: coming, being with, and being sent out. After being sent out to serve him, the disciples return to be with him.

Spend time meditating on verses 28-30 today. What phrase or word stands out and holds your attention? Stay with that word or phrase, and reflect on it in the quiet.

Allow it to sink into all corners of your life. Journal your responses to God's teaching.

[DAY 6]
Responding through Reflection
As you reflect over this week, ask the Holy Spirit to help you see your week as God does. Ask the Lord to show you where he has been present in your life—with you or in others.

Take some time to reflect on your inner attitudes and feelings. Pay attention to your experiences of love, joy, harmony, freedom. Take note of any experiences of pain, confusion, anger, anxiety, or entrapment.

How is God speaking to you, drawing you, in these experiences? In what ways are you responding to or cooperating with God? In what ways are you not?

What is your prayer now? Is it confession, praise, thanksgiving, petition, intercession?

Preparing for Your Time Together
In your time together with your spiritual friend, take some time to quiet yourselves and to be present to God and to each other. Then share with each other how God has been present to you this week and how you are responding. Is there a place you sense the need to focus your attention on, to pray more about, or to take action on?

What are those places where you need each other's prayer support about specific areas of inner change, resistance, or growth as you keep moving on the outward journey?

Dealing with Conflict

[··]

PRAYER FOCUS
*Lord, I take your gentle yoke upon me
and learn from you.*

COMING
Take some time to place your body, mind, and spirit into the presence of God. Use an exercise from PART THREE if you find one helpful.

BEING WITH
Here and there in our journey through Matthew's Gospel, we have seen the Pharisees and the teachers of the Law standing off to themselves, criticizing Jesus and his followers. In this twelfth chapter, the tension begins to mount. The merciful righteousness and faithfulness to which Jesus

calls us (5:20) come into conflict with the legalism of the Pharisees.

On DAY 5 last week, our meditation was centered in Jesus' invitation to come and take his yoke upon us. This week we will be seeing the kind of yoke the religious rulers laid on people.

At the end of each BEING WITH time, stay in the presence of Jesus and meditate on his yoke and what it means to you. Talk with Jesus about it. Listen to him. Record your learnings in your journal.

[DAY 1]
Freedom versus guilt
MATTHEW 12:1-8

As you read the story, reflect on where this event happens and who is there. Listen to the conversation.

What do you learn about the yoke of the Pharisees (vv. 2, 7)? What do you learn about the easy yoke of Jesus?

Use these words of Jesus as a prayer of meditation:

Come to me, all of you who are tired from carrying heavy loads, and I will give you rest. Take my yoke and put it on you, and learn from me, because I am gentle and humble in spirit; and you will find rest. For the yoke I will give you is easy, and the load I will put on you is light.
—Matthew 11:28-30 , TEV

Journal the insights and learnings from your meditation.

[DAY 2]
Helping versus legalism
MATTHEW 12:9-14

It is still the sabbath. We walk away from the wheat fields and over to the synagogue, still with Jesus and his disciples. As you sit in the synagogue, you notice a man with a paralyzed hand. Enter further into the story—listen, see, feel, touch.

Again you are confronted with the contrast between the yoke of the Pharisees, with their legalistic view of what makes a person righteous before God, and the kind yoke of Jesus. Reflect on the differences between the two.

Meditate in prayer using the passage above from DAY 1. Journal your learnings and your experience.

[DAY 3]
Gentleness in response to rejection
MATTHEW 12:15-21

A number of times in our journey through Matthew, we have withdrawn with Jesus to escape from places where there were threats on his life (2:13-14, 22-23; 4:12). Now Jesus withdraws again. In their desire for power, the Pharisees are unable to yield control to God, and they begin to make plans to kill Jesus. This is their way of taking control. But Jesus walks under the yoke of his heavenly Father. It is out of this relationship that Jesus responds.

As you meditate on this passage, what more do you discover about the easy yoke of Jesus? about the gentleness of justice and hope?

In your prayer meditation use the yoke passage again and journal your insights from the meditation.

[DAY 4]
For Jesus or against
MATTHEW 12:22-32

If the Pharisees see themselves as servants of God, then from their perspective, Jesus must be a servant of Satan. And so, Jesus is finally accused of being a tool in the hands of Satan.

The yokes that we accept and allow to control our understanding of reality can be deadly or life-giving. In verses 31-32, Jesus points out the danger of being weighed down under a yoke that refuses to allow the Holy Spirit to breathe truth and freedom into our thinking. The work of the Spirit is vital to our knowing God, to our being brought into the kingdom. If we reject the spirit of God (the spirit described in verse 18, the spirit that rests upon Jesus), we reject God's way of bringing us to God; we reject forgiveness of our sin.

After reading the passage prayerfully several times, spend some time in prayer using the yoke passage from DAY 1. Then journal your insights and impressions.

[DAY 5]
Good treasure versus bad treasure
MATTHEW 12:33-37

Jesus draws us again and again to look within—at our heart. What fills our heart will spill over into what we say and do.

The righteousness of the Pharisees denies there is evil within. The greater faithfulness and righteousness is honest about our heart problem. Under the yoke of Jesus, we are freed to be honest about ourselves, and we are met with kindness and grace. This is the good news: Jesus came to call sinners to himself (9:12-13).

"Happy are those who know they are spiritually poor; the Kingdom of heaven belongs to them!" he told the crowds on the mountain (5:3, TEV).

The judgment referred to in this passage (vv. 36-37) has to do with words—the outward sign of what is in the heart. As we listen to what we say, we discover what is within.

Jesus calls us to begin discerning where our words and actions come from. Always remember: He meets us with grace and mercy. Living under his yoke will begin to sensitize us to what is within.

In your prayer time, use the yoke passage from DAY 1. Journal your learnings.

[DAY 6]
Responding through Reflection

As you come into the quiet today, be gentle with yourself in the presence of Jesus. His yoke is easy, kind, and light. And he will give you rest.

Ask the Lord to show you where he has been present in your life—with you or in others.

Take some time to reflect on your inner attitudes and feelings. Pay attention to your experiences of love, joy, harmony, or freedom. Note any experiences of pain, confusion, anger, anxiety, or entrapment.

How is God speaking to you, drawing you, in these experiences?

In what ways are you responding to or cooperating with God? In what ways are you not?

What is your prayer now—confession, praise, thanksgiving, petition, intercession?

Preparing for Your Time Together

Listen gently and carefully to each other as you share your learnings from this week about Jesus' yoke and your inner heart. Listen prayerfully to what God is saying to you and how you are responding to God.

Where are those places you are sensing a need to focus attention, to pray over, to take action on?

Learning to Trust in Times of Crisis

[··]

Lord, help me to recognize you in times of crisis.

COMING

You are continuing in the rhythm of coming, being with, and going out. This is the time of coming—of walking away from activity to be with God. Settle yourself in God's presence. Use a prayer exercise if you find one helpful.

BEING WITH

Meditation . . . is alternately "a dance" and "a fight," or else it is both at once. But we continually turn to it for renewal and to find tranquility after the rush and worry of action. I refer not only to the worry that arises from our sinful lusts, but also that which is inseparable from even the sincerest vocation of service . . . Meditation makes us independent of events, by making us dependent upon God.[41]

[DAY 1]
Trust is hearing and understanding.
MATTHEW 13:1-9, 18-23

The parable about the sower and the seed is about four different soils. As we dig a bit deeper into what Jesus was saying, we realize that the soils are four different ways of hearing God:

The seed on the path represents those who hear and don't understand. The evil one snatches away what they hear (vv. 4, 19).

The rocky ground represents those who hear, but the word does not sink deeply into them (vv. 5, 20). When trouble comes, they give up quickly.

The thorn bushes speak of a person who hears but the worry about this life and a love for riches chokes off any growth (vv. 7, 22).

The seed in good soil is for those who hear and understand—and bear fruit (vv. 8, 23).

Trust in God is closely tied to how we hear and understand. Take some time in your meditation on this text to listen to what God is sowing in your heart. Such meditation allows the word of God to sink into the soil of our heart and bear fruit.

Journal your insights and learnings.

[DAY 2]
Trust is giving up control.
MATTHEW 14:1-21

The outward journey of obedience will lead us to places where our trust in God and God's greater purpose and reality, will help us find meaning in the face of loss and in the face of our human weakness.

After he hears of John's death, Jesus withdraws. But even as he seeks the quiet of solitude, the crowd is waiting for him. In response to the crowd's need for food at the end of the day, the disciples want nothing more than to avoid getting involved. But Jesus draws them back into the situation and presses them for a response.

Such situations strip us of our ability to cope on our own. Our resources are small, human, and limited (v. 17). The need here is for the disciples to realize that they do not have to have control. They do not need to cope alone.

Discounting what they have is one way of having control (vv. 16, 17). Offering up what they have to Jesus releases their gifts and themselves to his control. The outcome is in his hands: He takes, he blesses, he breaks, and he gives. Jesus is helping them learn to trust.

In your contemplation of this story, walk into the event. Sit with the disciples and listen to the response to Jesus as he has compassion on the multitude (vv. 14-15).

What does he ask from you? What do you have to give? Note in your journal what you are learning about trust and about control.

[DAY 3]
Trust is susceptible to bouts of "little faith."
MATTHEW 14:22-33

Once again, obeying Jesus has brought his disciples to a fearful, stormy place. Jesus has been encountering his own inner and outer storms (14:1-3, 10-13, 22-23). Now he comes to the disciples who had done his bidding and found the wind and waves against them (v. 24). They are terrified.

> The life of discipleship is susceptible to bouts of little faith .... Nevertheless, Jesus does not abandon his disciples at

such times but stands ever ready with his saving power to sustain them so that they can in fact discharge the mission he has entrusted to them.[42]

As you contemplate this story, place yourself in the event. What are the boat and the storm for you? Who is Jesus for you in this (vv. 28, 30, 33)? Where do you find yourself experiencing bouts of "little faith"? Journal your insights.

[DAY 4]
Trust is walking in freedom.
MATTHEW 15:1-9

If we are honest with ourselves, we have a deep need to please others. When pleasing others comes into conflict with following and obeying Christ, we can feel caught in a dilemma. Jesus helps us discern between human rules and his word (v. 9). As you meditate on this story, what is God saying to you? Journal your response.

[DAY 5]
Trust is the freedom to expose what is within.
MATTHEW 15:10-20

Jesus brings us back once again to where the real problem is: within us. Only he can set us free from our inner self (Romans 5:1-5). He came to be with us and he came to rescue us from the slavery of sin (1:21, 23).

As you meditate on these scriptures, stay with the word or phrase that holds your attention. Allow it to sink into your thinking, understanding, and your inner self. Journal your awareness and learnings.

[DAY 6]
Responding through Reflection

As you look back over your week and your journal entries, do you find any patterns emerging? What are you learning about yourself? about trust? about Jesus?

Ask God to show you where he has been present in your life—with you or in others.

Take some time to reflect on your inner attitudes and feelings. Pay attention to your experiences of love, joy, harmony, and freedom. Note any experiences of pain, confusion, anger, anxiety, or entrapment.

How is God speaking to you, drawing you, in these experiences? What is your prayer just now—confession, praise, thanksgiving, petition, intercession?

Preparing for Your Time Together
Begin listening for patterns in each other's lives. Maybe you will not see one; we cannot make happen what is not there. Be listening for each other's trust in God and your response to God out of that trust.

Learning to Think the Thoughts of God

[··]

PRAYER FOCUS
Lord, help me to think the thoughts of God.

COMING
Take some time to bring your body, mind, and spirit into the quiet presence of God. Allow any busy thoughts to slip away; rest any heavy thoughts in God's presence.

BEING WITH
One of the tasks of discipleship is to distinguish truth from untruth. Jesus speaks of this as thinking the things of God as opposed to thinking the things of humankind (16:23). We find Jesus continually discerning both the distance and

the difference between the two and teaching his disciples to discern as he does.

[DAY 1]
What feeds my thoughts?
MATTHEW 13:33; 16:5-12

A woman began a dialogue with God. One of the first needs she admitted was her desire to know God more closely. She further admitted that she felt far from God. Then she listened. The response she heard from God was this: "Maybe you should give up reading the newspaper for an hour after breakfast. Maybe you should spend that time with me."

At first she was surprised that God spoke. And then she pondered what God said. She decided to listen to God's advice and to read the newspaper at another time in the day. After breakfast became the time when she spent time with God and listened to God. Her relationship with God grew, and she began to read the newspaper with new insight.

In the quiet, get in touch with your own desire for God. Dialogue with God about it.

[DAY 2]
Retreat in the mountains
MATTHEW 16:13-20

Climb the mountain with Jesus and his other disciples today. As you sit on the grassy slopes, listen to Jesus' questions. What is your answer? Who is Jesus for you?

We know the answer Peter gave, but what is the answer that grows out of our own experience of walking with Jesus and having him walk with us?

Journal your awarenesses of your walk with Jesus.

[DAY 3]
Following means suffering.
MATTHEW 16:21-28

Stay on the mountain today and reflect deeply as you hear Jesus telling you the cost of following him. What kind of thoughts do you hear within yourself? What is the cross for you (v. 24)?

Be honest before God in your journal, and bring your responses to him. Then seek to discern whether they are from God or from your human nature.

[DAY 4]
Listening
MATTHEW 17:1-13, 22-23

We are allowed to join Peter, James, and John as Jesus leads them up another high mountain. There, away from the crowds, in the quiet of the mountain, God meets with them.

> Guided retreats and quiet days . . . . encourage both intimate relaxation and struggle with the Real One welling up in and around us. They can offer protected respites from the breathless driveness [sic] of culture and ego.[43]

We can get caught up in the spiritual experience for itself and overlook God, who is present. God stills the clutching excitement of the disciples as he draws their attention back to listening to Jesus. Be present to Jesus now. Simply be attentive and listen. Journal your listenings.

[DAY 5]
Thinking the thoughts of God
ROMANS 12:1-2

As you meditate on these words, reflect also on what Jesus says about the shape of discipleship (Matthew 16:24-27), both its cost and its rewards. We carry a cross and live in hope—walking like Jesus in the greater reality of the resurrection (v. 21) and Jesus' second coming. Journal your listenings.

[DAY 6]
Responding through Reflection
Reflect today on what you have been hearing this week.

Ask the Lord to show you where God has been present in your life—with you or in others.

Take some time to reflect on your inner attitudes and feelings. Pay attention to your experiences of love, joy, harmony, or freedom. Note any experiences of pain, confusion, anger, anxiety, or entrapment.

How is God speaking to you, drawing you, in these experiences? What is your prayer today?

Preparing for Your Time Together
In your time with your spiritual friend, share from your prayer experiences this week. How are you learning to "think the thoughts of God"? What blocks are you discovering that hinder your responding to God?

Downward Mobility

[··]

PRAYER FOCUS
Lord, help me to see as you see.

COMING
Take a few minutes to bring yourself into God's presence.

BEING WITH

Whoever wishes to become great among you must be your servant, and whoever wishes to be first among you must be slave of all. For the Son of Man came not to be served but to serve, and to give his life a ransom for many.[44]

[DAY 1]
Letting go of control: Making space to receive
MATTHEW 18:6-14

Jesus shifts his focus from the child (vv. 1-5) to the children who believe in him—his followers. Our return to God and our belonging in God's household is the reason Jesus came among us.

Hence the startling anger and seriousness with which Jesus warns the one who places a stumbling block in the path of our journey to and with God: whether another person or our own lifestyle choices (vv. 6-9). We are to search for the one who does stumble and fall until that one is found and restored (vv. 10-14).

As you meditate prayerfully on this passage, what word or phrase catches your attention? Stay with it and allow the word or phrase to sink gently into the rooms and relationships of your life. Journal your response to God.

[DAY 2]
Letting go of revenge: Being receptive to restoration
MATTHEW 18:15-35

We go to our brother or sister who wrongs us, not to condemn or get even, but to restore the relationship—to make peace (5:9). We cannot control the response of the other person (vv. 16-17), but we are instructed to guard our own attitude (vv. 21-22, 35).

It may be that you feel some hesitation or distance between yourself and your spiritual friend or between you and another person in the community of faith. As you wait in God's presence, bring that person and yourself to God. What resistance do you discover within yourself? What desire for peace is there, if any? Make a note of your reflection in your journal.

[DAY 3]
Letting go of ego: Empowering the powerless
MATTHEW 19:1-15

After being in retreat in the mountains, Jesus and his disciples journey south. In the presence of God, he receives strength and direction. Now they begin the long walk to Jerusalem.

On the road he is met by Pharisees who come to test him with a question: May a man divorce his wife for any cause? (At that time a man could divorce his wife for burning his evening meal.) Jesus looks beyond the narrow and hard attitude present in the question and in the male view of women. He points to God's creation of both men and women and in so doing reminds his hearers of the image of God within our person, in both women and men.

As children are brought to Jesus for his blessing, the disciples forget the lesson he has just taught them (18:1-5). He rebukes their hasty response and with simple hospitality makes space for the children. Jesus embraces and blesses the powerless.

Place yourself in the story, join the disciples on the road to Jerusalem. Who do you find yourself standing close to? What do you need from Jesus? Who are the powerless you can bless in your life? Journal your insights and learnings.

[DAY 4]
Giving up those things that prevent us from following
MATTHEW 19:16-30

Now a young man comes up to Jesus and asks how to receive eternal life. Jesus finally puts his finger on the one thing that is a stumbling block in the path of this man's journey to God: the young man's wealth (v. 21).

As you wait in the presence of Jesus, ask him: "What do you think of my life? What stumbling blocks do you see?" Journal your listenings.

[DAY 5]
Downward mobility—to the cross
MATTHEW 20:17-28

Still the disciples are unable to recognize the face of greatness in the kingdom of heaven: serving others in the same way Jesus served and gave his life. What is downward mobility for you? Journal your insights.

[DAY 6]
Responding through Reflection

The closer we come to the cross, the more we are confronted with the parts of our lives that need to be laid down out of love for Jesus. Place yourself on the road to Jerusalem with Jesus today. Walk with him, listen to him. Reflect on what you have learned from him this week.

Ask the Lord to show you where God has been present in your life—with you or in others. Take some time to reflect on your inner attitudes and feelings. Note your experiences of love, joy, harmony, and freedom. Pay attention to any experiences of pain, confusion, anger, anxiety, or entrapment.

How is God speaking to you, drawing you, in these experiences? What is your prayer today?

Preparing for Your Time Together

From time to time you may be feeling some distance, some hesitation between you and your spiritual friend. Bring this gently into the space between you today, along with your prayer experience. Listen carefully to each other as you share what God is saying to you and reflect on how you are each responding to God.

Journey to the Cross

[··]

PRAYER FOCUS
Lord, help me to stay with you.

COMING
Relax; be still and attentive in God's presence.

BEING WITH
"You will name him Jesus—because he will save his
people from their sins" (Matthew 1:21, TEV).

[DAY 1]
"Your king is coming."
MATTHEW 21:1-17

As you enter Jerusalem with Jesus, notice who is present
and what their responses are to Jesus. Where do you find
yourself standing? Who do you find yourself identifying

with? Note in your journal something of your prayer experience.

[DAY 2]
"I wanted, but you would not."
MATTHEW 23:37-39; 26:1-16

Throughout the story at this point, Matthew traces two distinct movements for us: One is the mounting rejection fueling the plot against Jesus' life; the other is the steady love of Jesus for God and for people as he walks toward the cross.

Enter the story slowly, prayerfully. Stay in the place where you find yourself meeting Jesus. Journal your prayer experience.

[DAY 3]
"This is my blood . . .
poured out for the forgiveness of sins."
MATTHEW 26:17-35

Like so many mealtimes before, Jesus takes the bread, gives thanks, breaks it, and gives it. This is the last time before the cross and the breaking of his body. Then he takes the wine, gives thanks, and gives it to his disciples. He tells them it is his blood and that it seals the new covenant. The old covenant is fulfilled; the new one begins.

Jesus knows our weaknesses, our capacity to betray him (v. 31), but he invites us to meet him in Galilee (v. 32). We are always welcomed back. Jesus' giving of himself has made a way for us to come.

[DAY 4]
"Not what I want but what you want."
MATTHEW 26:36–56

Obedience costs. But when we say, "Yet not what I want, but what you want," we are not alone. Jesus has knelt on that ground too. But, as he did, we may well walk in that obedience alone (vv. 31, 57).

Walk quietly in the story today. Wait in the garden in the presence of God. What is your prayer? Who is Jesus for you? You may want to journal your prayer today.

[DAY 5]
"Truly this man was God's Son."
MATTHEW 27:27-61

Stripped, made fun of, spat upon, led out, crucified. Accused, insulted, mocked by the people, abandoned by God. Jesus gave a loud cry and breathed his last.

When Jesus gave himself on the cross, in seeming weakness, the centurion became convinced that Jesus was who he was: God's son.

Sit before the cross today. Watch and wait.

[DAY 6]
Responding Through Reflection

As you come into the quiet today, ask the Holy Spirit to help you see your week as God does.

For what are you thankful? Where have you seen God—in others, in the larger world, in yourself?

How is God drawing you near in your experiences of love, joy, and harmony? in your experiences of pain, confusion, anger, or anxiety?

In what ways are you responding to God?

Preparing for Your Time Together

Reflect carefully on what you would like to share about your prayer and life experience this week. Be listening for what God is saying and for how you are responding.

Soon the three-month journey will be complete. Pray and talk together about whether you desire to continue walking together or not.

Jesus Christ with Us until the End of the Age

[··]

PRAYER FOCUS
Lord, help me to live in faith, hope, and love.

COMING
Gently relax and allow any tension to fall away as you open yourself to God's presence with you.

BEING WITH

He will be called Emmanuel (which means "God is with us").   —Matthew 1:23, TEV

Go, then, to all peoples. And I will be with you always, to the end of the age.   —Matthew 28:19-20, TEV

Week 13

[DAY 1]
The risen Jesus is with you always.
MATTHEW 28:1-20

The eleven are commissioned by Jesus to go on the great outward journey. Beginning in Jerusalem and moving out into the world, they walk under the authority of Jesus Christ and the greater reality of God's kingdom to make disciples of all nations. From those early days after the resurrection on down through the centuries, one faithful disciple told first one and then another, and so the message has come to us today.

Think of those persons who link your faith journey to the journey of those early women and men and take a moment to thank God for their faithfulness.

Spend some time reflecting on your own outward journey. What is the risen Jesus nudging you to do? Where does this outward journey take you?

Remember that even in the journey of your searching for direction, Jesus is "with you always, to the end of the age."

[DAY 2]
Living in hope in the present age
MATTHEW 24:3-14

The disciples asked Jesus about the present age: How long would it last? What would be the sign of Jesus' return and of the end of this age?

We live in a world of chaotic political upheavals, with "nation [rising] against nation, and kingdom against kingdom" and there are "famines and earthquakes in various places" (v. 7). Jesus foresaw these events and told his followers about them but drew their attention away from being alarmed in the midst of the chaos—for the chaos is not the end. Jesus is Lord of the end, and "the end is not yet" (v. 8). He goes on to describe what will happen to those who are faithful, and what the state of the world will become "because of the increase of lawlessness" (v. 12). But again, he draws our attention away from the violence and anarchy to simple faithfulness to Jesus Christ and to the proclamation of the good news in all the world. Then the end will come (v. 14).

Jesus is not instructing his followers to ignore war, violence, and chaos; to somehow remove themselves from the pain and terrible anxiety people live in from day to day. Rather, he is calling us not to be controlled by what seems chaotic and uncontrollable but to stay with him in simple trust.

Julian of Norwich lived in England during a century of tumult and crisis: great schisms in the church, the Hundred Years' War between England and France, the chaos of the Peasants' Revolt, and even the overruning of Norwich itself by rebels. Through all of this, she stayed close to God, and could say:

> Just so [our Lord] said in the last words, with perfect fidelity, alluding to us all: You will not be overcome . . . . And these words: You will not be overcome, were said very insistently and strongly, for certainty and strength against every tribulation which may come. He did not say: You will not be troubled, you will not be belaboured, you will not be disquieted; but he said: You will not be overcome.[45]

Reflect quietly on Julian's listenings and on where you find your hope in the face of world chaos.

[DAY 3]
Watching in faith for his coming
MATTHEW 24:29-31, 36-44

The disciples asked Jesus when he would return. And down through the years many persons have sought to set a date. But Jesus draws our attention away from date-setting (v. 36) and helps us understand that such knowledge is not available to us. Rather, he calls us to be faithful and to "stay awake" (v. 42).

The faithful practice of spiritual disciplines helps us to be aware of God, to be awake to where God is present, and to recognize how we are responding. Gradually our hearts are emptied of the clutter of the world that we think we have to have for our happiness and security, and we have an open space for hope, love, and faithfulness to grow and be at home. We will notice an intensifying in our longing for his return and to see him as he is (1 John 3:2-3).

As you meditate on these teachings of Jesus, what words or phrases stand out for you? Stay with these words, let them settle into your heart and life.

[DAY 4]
Being faithful until he comes
MATTHEW 25:1-30

Notice that the master gives the talents, entrusting what was his to the servants. Jesus describes two responses: Two servants were faithful; one was afraid and simply buried his talent in the earth.

The parable is designed for us to reflect on gifts—some large, some small; the Giver; our use of the gifts while we wait for the Master's return; being trustworthy with what we have; and the joy of the Master.

All of what we have and are is a gift from God. We are simply stewards; God is the owner.

Spend some time in quiet in God's presence after asking the question: Lord, in what way do I live and serve to bring you joy? Journal your listenings.

[DAY 5]
Caring for members of Christ's family
MATTHEW 25:31-46

In various places in Matthew, Jesus has emphasized his solidarity with those who follow him. "Whoever does the will of my Father in heaven is my brother and sister and mother" (12:50). He calls his disciples members "of his household" (10:24). Jesus so identifies with his followers as they live and serve in this present age that the person who welcomes them, gives them something to eat or drink, clothes them or takes care of them while they are sick, or visits them in prison is welcomed: "Come, you that are blessed by my Father!" (25:34). Some will be truly surprised. While serving a simple meal or making space in their lives and home for the unexpected visitor who is Christ's brother or sister, they have made space for Jesus.

So we are to be on the lookout for strangers, for the most humble of his sisters and brothers, and for angels— those messengers who are followers of Jesus. Such hospitality allows Jesus in and is a blessing to us, to the one we welcome, and to God. This is one of the shapes of faithfulness until Jesus comes—making space for people to be fed, clothed, cared for, and visited when ill or in prison.

When the phone rang in their apartment in Frankfurt, Germany, the young wife was not happy to hear that she and her husband were to receive company from Czechoslovakia that weekend. All the other mission workers would be away for several days. Reluctantly she and her husband agreed, wondering how they could make space in an already overcrowded, three-room apartment.

When Ernst Schmucker arrived, his radiant smiling face, his gentle presence, and his deep inner joy breathed light and hope into the lives of the two tired mission workers. Ernst had endured the communist takeover of his country, frequent interrogations, and constant surveillance. He lived in the hope and the joy of Jesus' coming. As he told his story, the children and their parents listened and rejoiced with him.

One afternoon, while Ernst was out for a visit in the city, the little four-year-old son woke up from his nap and wandered into the kitchen. "Where's Jesus?" he asked.

"Jesus?" responded his mother.

"Yes, Jesus. Where's the Jesus man?" he asked again.

The young mother smiled and felt a deep sense of joy and strength springing up within her. How glad she was that they had said, "Yes, Mr. Schmucker can come."

As you reflect on Jesus' teaching, who are the "angels" who have shown up at your door or in your life? How did you respond?

[DAY 6]
Response through Reflection

Spiritual friendship is a profound act of hospitality. As we graciously receive each other, we are also looking for God in our journeys. And as we begin to see God in each other, we become aware of God in those around us and in the larger world.

What kind of encouragement do you need to be faithful in this present age? How has meeting with a spiritual friend helped you? How has God been showing up in your times of quiet and in the rest of your life this week?

Preparing for Your Time Together

After a time of quiet prayer, take time to listen to each other's journey and experience of the last three months. Be present and receptive to each other as you explore what you need as you continue on your journey in this present age.

What helps you to be aware of Jesus' presence with you (28:20)? In what ways are you ready to continue meeting with a spiritual friend? In what ways are you not? What commitments are you open to exploring?

PART FIVE

Ongoing
Spiritual Friendship

[··]

CHAPTER 14

The Next Step

[··]

No relationship is static, and all our relationships, insofar as they are under the guidance of the Holy Spirit, move more and more towards spiritual friendship. They move in that direction simply because this is the kind of God Christians believe in . . . . . God is friendship. We are made after [God's] image.[46]

If you have traveled this far with a spiritual friend or a small group, you may be wondering about ongoing spiritual friendship. This little guide based on Matthew's Gospel is only one of many different ways of setting some kind of structure for your time together. You may have some idea of what you would like to focus on next.

During the times of reading, reflection, and sharing, some discover an area of their lives that needs attention. Sometimes there is just a sense of the need to continue. Either way, God is nudging us on. This call of God is our highest adventure. It is on this journey that we will know our greatest battles and our fullest joys.

While the scriptures do not place the battle at the center—only Jesus can ever hold that place in God's great reality—even a casual reading of the biblical account makes it clear to us that knowing God and living in harmony with God is no easy task. We are confronted with enemies from without and from within.[47] However, God has not planned for us to journey alone, even though in the deepest sense, our journey is only our own. We cannot journey for another. But the companionship of another who is also walking in the Way is both comforting and strengthening. The presence of others who are in the believing community is for our good.[48]

If you are unsure as to your next step, listen prayerfully to your inner heart and spirit and open yourself to God's gentle guidance. Are there entries in your journal that you would like to explore more fully with a spiritual friend? What needs are you aware of? What longings do you hear?

You may decide to continue for a time—maybe to covenant to walk together for a year—with the person with whom you explored Matthew's Gospel. You may decide you would like to share your journey with another.

[··]

One woman discovered a readiness to look more closely at her personal pilgrimage. She sensed God was inviting her to walk further on her inward journey. Such exploration is often accompanied by an openness to be more present to another, and she invited a friend to consider a mutual journey into their respective childhoods, paying attention to pain, dysfunction, comfort, and strengths.

These women trusted God's gentle, healing presence to accompany them as they chose a book to read and met weekly to hear each other's discoveries.

One man became aware of his need for more time in prayer and solitude as he began practicing spiritual disciplines during the course. He wondered how to balance his schedule of work, family, and church involvement to include the space he desired for being present to God. But he also wondered about his identity: Where did he look for affirmation and acceptance—to other men and their production-filled life or to God? What if someone asked him about his schedule, and he admitted he needed more time for prayer? Would he be understood? What did this tug on his inner person mean? He decided to explore these questions and others with a spiritual friend.

Another woman felt God's inviting her to respond to the movement of God's presence in her life by writing to a friend and asking her to enter into spiritual friendship with her. At first her friend was hesitant, but as the first woman continued to write and to explain what she was learning and appreciating about such a relationship, the friend agreed. These women correspond regularly. In their letters they include whatever they feel comfortable sharing from their journals, prayer requests, and responses to some of the questions included in *Guidelines for a Spiritual Friendship*.[49] They try to meet together every three months.

Two other women meet about every three weeks. One is beginning to share what she is discovering as she learns to pray out of her experiences. For years she had begun her prayers where she thought God and the church wanted her to be. Now, as a widow who is adjusting to living alone and to taking more responsibility for practical, everyday, and business decisions, she is finding a new restfulness as she discovers and relates to God's presence in her daily experience and her responses to the everyday. The other woman is seeking God's direction as she listens to nudgings in her life to leave her present vocation and return to school. Both women find a common bond as they share their experiences of transition and change.

A husband and wife set aside an hour and a half a week to wait in God's presence in silent prayer, then to journal their respective listenings. During the last half-hour, they listen attentively as they read their journal entries to each other.

Two men meet about once a month to discuss what they are receiving through the reading of other spiritual writers and how their relationships at work, in their families, and with God are being touched.

One woman finds that as she makes regular hospital visits to a family member during an extended life-threatening illness, she is learning to listen as a spiritual friend and is more able to be present to the pain, uncertainty, and waiting along with others in the hospital who also wait.

Two male students committed themselves to meet for lunch once a week. Their main focus was to assist each other to remember to be present to God in the tight schedule between work, seminary classes, readings, assignments, and family responsibilities.

Two mothers of teenage children meet together at a quiet table in a coffee shop once a week to be gently accountable to each other. Their conversation as spiritual friends includes how they are living out their love for God, for themselves, and for their children-becoming-adults. They too use the *Guidelines for a Spiritual Friendship* as a starting point and move out from there.

A group of women who live and serve in mission work in several different countries around the world acknowledged their need for support and for spiritual friendship. Besides the group letters that the women write each month, each woman paired up with another to be spiritual friends to each other. Two of these women agreed to pray for each other daily, to write once a month, and to meet for a weekend of retreat once a quarter. The days for retreat include time for meditation on scripture, silent prayer, journaling, and sharing their journals and journeys together.[50]

Two men meet once a week for seventy-five minutes to read and meditate on the coming Sunday's lectionary reading, using *lectio divina* as a way of allowing the scripture to move from their head into their hearts and lives.

[··]

A number of good resources are becoming available to assist us in our spiritual formation. If you find that your needs are slightly different from those of your spiritual friend, you may decide to read separate books but agree to meet to companion each other on your journeys.

In all of our journeying, our primary spiritual guide is the Holy Spirit. The spirit of Jesus will continue to create the quiet center within us—the place of meeting, of being listened to, of listening, and of restful companionship.

[··]

If you love me, you will keep my commandments. And I will ask the Father, and he will give you another Advocate, to be with you forever. This is the Spirit of truth, whom the world cannot receive, because it neither sees him nor knows him. You know him, because he abides with you, and he will be in you.[51]

[*APPENDIX*]

Guidelines for Basic Spiritual Friendship

THESE GUIDELINES ARE USED BY *students at Associated Mennonite Biblical Seminaries in Elkhart, Indiana, and at Eastern Mennonite Seminary in Harrisonburg, Virginia. They were developed in September of 1989 by Marcus Smucker, Marlene Kropf, and Erland Waltner, faculty members who teach and give spiritual direction at AMBS. The author is grateful for their permission to reprint them.*

PREPARATION
1. Arrange for time, place, length of session; agree upon who will be the focus of a session at any given time.
2. Pray for the sessions in advance asking God's direction. Pray regularly for one another.

PARTICIPATION

Shared Awareness
Begin the sessions with silence (2 to 3 minutes).

Shared Presence
1. Be attentive to your friend. Listen . . .
Openly—rather than being immediately directive.
Compassionately—rather than being too corrective.
Reflectively—rather than being compulsive.
With observations—rather than too many conclusions.
With clarifying questions—rather than being closed or curious.
2. Be attentive to God's workings in each other's life by reflecting together upon questions such as:
How has God been at work in my life this week?
What have been the signs of God's grace to me?
What images/awareness of God has been helpful to me?
What may have blocked God's voice to me this week?
Where might I have failed to experience God's grace?

What sin do I need to confess?
3. Be attentive to God's immediate presence in your friend's life
   by asking reflective questions such as. . .
   How is God being with you now?
   What is God saying to you now?
   How is God motivating/energizing/transforming you?
   How are you responding to God in your life now?
Encourage time for "waiting" before the Lord.

Shared Commitments

Be attentive to your friend's need for accountability by asking:
   What decisions do I want and need to make in the week to
   come?
   What action to take, prayers to pray, reflection to do?
   What changes are being called for in my life?
   For what do I want and need to be held accountable till we
   meet again?

Shared Closure

Prayers of acknowledgment, confession, petition, silence,
thanksgiving, and intercession.

Additional Areas Upon Which You May Focus

Sharing in the spiritual friendship could include:
   My spiritual pilgrimage.
   My experience of God.
   My images of (names for, and how I see) God.
   My patterns of communication with God (prayer experience).
   My relationship with others or with the church.
   How I experience the world.
   Areas for spiritual growth in my life.

[*NOTES*]

1. Acts 9:10-19.
2. Acts 9:26-28.
3. Acts 8:26-35.
4. Psalm 42:1-2.
5. Tilden Edwards, *Spiritual Friend: Reclaiming the Gift of Spiritual Direction* (New York: Paulist Press, 1981) p.16.
6. Philippians 1:6; 2:13.
7. Romans 12:1-2; Galatians 4:19; 5:16-26; Philippians 2:5ff.
8. Eugene H. Peterson, *Working the Angles: The Shape of Pastoral Integrity* (Michigan: Eerdmans Publishing Co., 1987), p. 104.
9. Margaret Guenther, "Attending to the Holy," address given at the Spiritual Directors' International Symposium, Baltimore, MD, May 1992. She expands the idea of attention to God in a recent book *Holy Listening: The Art of Spiritual Direction* (Cowley Publications, 1992).
10. Edwards, *Spiritual Friend*, p. 101.
11. Ibid., p. 101–102.
12. Andrew Murray, ed., *Freedom from a Self-Centered Life: Dying to Self* (Minnesota: Dimension Books, 1977), pp. 21-22. Selections from the writings of William Law.
13. Edwards, *Spiritual Friend*, p. 121.
14. Ibid., p. 105.
15. Peterson, *Working the Angles*, p. 118.
16. Aelred of Rievaulx, "Marriage and the Contemplative Life," *Spiritual Friendship* (Washington, D.C.: Consortium Press, 1974).
17. Edwards, *Spiritual Friend*, p. 121.
18. Ibid., p. 129.
19. Marcus Smucker, Marlene Kropf, Erland Waltner, "Guidelines for Spiritual Friendship," Associated Mennonite Biblical Seminaries, 1989.
20. William A. Barry, SJ, *Finding God in All Things: A Companion to the Spiritual Exercises of St. Ignatius* (Indiana: Ave Maria Press, 1991), p. 21.
21. Luke 5:8-10.
22. John 14:8, 9.

23. First John 4:10.
24. Matthew 1:23; 28:20.
25. Richard J. Foster, *Celebration of Discipline: The Path to Spiritual Growth* (New York: HarperCollins Publishers, 1988), p. 1.
26. Ibid., p. 7.
27. A. W. Tozer, *Man, The Dwelling Place of God* (Pennsylvania: Christian Publications, Inc., 1966), p. 52.
28. Henri J. M. Nowen, *Clowning in Rome: Reflections on Solitude, Celibacy, Prayer, and Contemplation* (New York: Image Books, 1979), p. 103.
29. Mark 3:13,14, TODAY'S ENGLISH VERSION.
30. Matthew 6:6.
31. Tilden Edwards, *Living in the Presence: Disciplines for the Spiritual Heart* (New York: Harper & Row, 1987), p. 22.
32. Anne Broyles, *Journaling: A Spirit Journey* (Nashville, TN: The Upper Room, 1988), and Joseph F. Schmidt, *Praying Our Experiences* (Minnesota: Saint Mary's Press, 1989) are both helpful resources.
33. Matthew 7:13, 14.
34. Foster, *Celebration of Discipline*, p. 20.
35. *The Spiritual Exercises of St. Ignatius*, trans. Louis J. Puhl (Loyola University Press, 1968). A helpful companion to the *Spiritual Exercises* is *Finding God in All Things* by William A. Barry, SJ.
36. Foster, *Celebration of Discipline*, p. 29.
37. Elizabeth O'Connor, *Letters to Scattered Pilgrims* (New York: Harper & Row, 1979), p. 39.
38. Author unknown. Fifteenth-century poem.
39. Foster, *Celebration of Discipline*, pp. 54, 55.
40. Jack Dean Kingsbury, *Matthew as Story* (Pennsylvania: Fortress Press, 1986), p. 29.
41. Paul Tournier, *The Person Reborn* (New York: Harper & Row, 1966), pp.184–85.
42. Kingsbury, *Matthew as Story*, p. 134.
43. Edwards, *Spiritual Friend*, p. 95.
44. Mark 10:43-45.
45. Julian of Norwich, *Showings*, trans. by Edmund Colledge and James Walsh (New York: Paulist Press, 1978), p. 315.
46. Alan Jones, *Exploring Spiritual Direction: An Essay on Christian Friendship* (New York: HarperCollins, 1982), p. 4.
47. Ephesians 6:10-18; James 1:12-16; Matthew 15:10-20.
48. Ephesians 4:11-16.
49. Smucker, Kropf, Waltner, "Guidelines for Spiritual Friendship."

50. Linda Shelly, "A Support Circle," WMSC *Voice*, May 1991, pp. 1011, published by Women's Missionary and Service Commission of the Mennonite Church (Ohio: Bluffton).
51. John 14:15-17.

About the Author

WENDY MILLER is an associate campus pastor and part-time teacher at Eastern Mennonite Seminary. She is also the founder of the School for Spiritual Formation in the Virginia Mennonite Conference. Born in England, Ms. Miller is a retreat leader and a spiritual director for individuals, missionary groups, and seminary students.